NARRATIVE OF TWO VOYAGES
TO THE
RIVER SIERRA LEONE

T0347097

CASS LIBRARY OF AFRICAN STUDIES

TRAVELS AND NARRATIVES

No. 30

Editorial Adviser: JOHN RALPH WILLIS

NARRATIVE

OF

TWO VOYAGES

TO THE

RIVER SIERRA LEONE

DURING THE YEARS
1791—1793

PERFORMED BY

A. M. FALCONBRIDGE

Routledge
Taylor & Francis Group

LONDON AND NEW YORK

First published by
FRANK CASS AND COMPANY LIMITED

First edition	1794
Second edition	1802
New impression	1967

Published 2006 by Routledge
2 Park Square, Milton Park, Abingdon, Oxfordshire OX14 4RN
711 Third Avenue, New York, NY 10017

First issued in paperback 2014

Routledge is an imprint of the Taylor and Francis Group, an informa business

ISBN 13: 978-0-714-61146-4 (hbk)
ISBN 13: 978-0-415-76035-5 (pbk)

Publisher's Note
The publisher has gone to great lengths to ensure the quality of this reprint but
points out that some imperfections in the original may be apparent

NARRATIVE

OF

TWO VOYAGES

TO THE RIVER

SIERRA LEONE,

DURING THE

YEARS 1791---2---3,

PERFORMED BY

A. M. FALCONBRIDGE.

WITH A

Succinct account of the Diſtreſſes and proceedings
of that Settlement; a deſcription of the
Manners, Diverſions, Arts, Com-
merce, Cultivation, Cuſtom,
Puniſhments, &c.

And Every intereſting Particular relating to the
SIERRA LEONE COMPANY.

ALSO

The preſent State of the SLAVE TRADE in the
Weſt Indies, and the improbability of
its total Abolition.

THE SECOND EDITION.

LONDON.

Printed for L. I. Higham, N° 6, Chifwell Street.

MDCCCII.

PRICE 3s. 6d.

DEDICATION

Inhabitants of Bristol.

AFTER revolving in my mind a length of time, whofe protection I might folicit for the fubfequent pages, it ftrikes me, I may look up with more confidence to the City I proudly boaft to be a native of, than to any other quarter.

Permit me, therefore, to trefpafs on your patience for a fhort fpace, by entreating your Countenance, and Patronage, to a faithful and juft account of two voyages to the inhofpitable Coaft of Africa.— Chequered throughout with fuch a complication of difafters as I may venture to affirm have never yet attended any of my *dear Country Women,* and fuch as I fincerely hope they never may experience.

I will

I will not undertake to promife you either elegant or modifh diction; and all I fhall advance in my favour, is a rigid adherence to truth, which (without embellifhment) I am perfuaded will meet its juft reward from the Inhabitants of Briftol; whom I truft, will have the goodnefs to keep in mind the infancy of my pen, that the recollection may ferve for an apology, fhould they at any time catch me giving too much fcope to its reins.

May every defcription of happinefs attend the Inhabitants of Briftol, is the earneft prayer

Of their Townfwoman,

and moft devoted,

and obedient humble Servant,

ANNA MARIA ———.

BRISTOL, *Auguft* 1794.

PREFACE.

PREFACE.

THE Authoress will not imitate a thread-bare prevailing custom, viz. assure the Public, the following letters were written without any design or intention of sending them into the world; on the contrary, she candidly confesses having some idea of the kind when writing them, though her mind was not fully made up on the business until towards the beginning of April,—nay, for some time before then (from a consciousness of the inability of her pen) she had actually relinquished all thoughts of publishing them, which determination she certainly would have adhered to, if her will had not been overruled by the importunities of her friends.

In her first Voyage, she has given her reasons for going to Africa, described the incidents and occurrences she met with and (from occular observations) the manners, customs, &c. of the people inhabiting those places she visited,— she has also made an humble attempt to delineate their situations and qualities, with a superficial History, of the Peninsula of Sierra Leone and its environs, which she certainly would have enlarged upon during her second Voyage, had not Lieutenant Matthews, previous to her returning to England in 1791, taken the start of her, by publishing his voyage to that Country ;— that being the case, it would not only have been superfluous, but discovering more vanity than she could wish the World to suppose her possessed of, had she offered to tread in a path already travelled over by such an ingenious and masterly pen, to which she begs to refer the inquisitive reader.

This consideration and this alone, induced the Authoress to confine the letters of her last Voyage principally to the transactions and pro-

gress

gress *of a Colony, whose success or* downfall
*she is persuaded the Inhabitants, at least the
thinking part, of almost every civilized Country, must feel more or less interested about,*
and she is forely afflicted *to warn the reader
of an unpromising account which could not
be otherwise, unless she had done* violence to
veracity ;—*she is well aware Truth is often
unwelcome, and foresees many facts produced
to the World in the course of those letters
will not be acceptable to the ears of numbers ;—therefore, in vindication of herself,
she refers the Public to the whole* Court
of Directors of the Sierra Leone Company, *and hopes, if it be in their power,
either severally or collectively, to contradict*
one tittle *she has advanced, they will do so
in the most candid manner ;—for the Authoress is open to conviction, and if convicted on this occasion, she will, with all*
due *deference,* kiss the rod of correction.

LETTER

———————

LETTER I.

LONDON, *Jan.* 5, 1791.

My dear Friend,

THE time draws nigh when I muſt bid adieu to my native land, perhaps for ever! The thoughts of it damps my ſpirits more than you can imagine, but I am reſolved to ſummon all the fortitude I can, being conſcious of meriting the reproaches of my friends and relations, for having haſtily married as I did contrary to their wiſhes, and am determined rather than be an incumbrance on them, to accompany my huſband even to the wilds of *Africa*, whither he is now bound, and meet ſuch fate as awaits me in preference to any poſſible comfort I could receive from them.

Mr. Falconbridge is employed by the St. George's Bay Company to carry out ſome relief for a number of unfortunate people, both blacks and whites, whom Government

Government fent to the river Sierra
Leone, a few years fince, and who in
confequence of having had fome difpute
with the natives, are fcattered through
the country, and are juft now as I have
been told, in the moft deplorable condition.

He (Mr. Falconbridge) is likewife to
make fome arrangements for collecting
thofe poor creatures again, and forming
a fettlement which the company have in
contemplation to eftablifh, not only to
ferve them, but to be generally ufeful
to the natives.

Mr. Falconbridge, his brother Mr. W.
Falconbridge and myfelf, are to embark on board the Duke of Buccleugh,
Captain McLean, a fhip belonging to
Meffrs. John and Alexander Anderfon,
of Philpot Lane; thefe gentlemen I underftand, have a confiderable factory at a
place called Bance Ifland, fome diftance
up the river Sierra Leone, to which
ifland the fhip is bound.

The company have either fent, or are
to fend out a fmall cutter called the
Lapwing, to meet Mr. F——, on the
coaft, fhe carries the ftores for relieving
the people, &c.   This

This is all the information I can give you at prefent, refpecting my intended voyage, but as it is an unufual enter-prize for an Englifh woman, to vifit the coaft of Africa; and as I have ever flattered myfelf with poffeffing your friendfhip, you will no doubt like to hear from me, and I therefore intend giving you a full and circumftantial ac-count of every thing that does not ef-cape my notice, 'till I return to this blefs'd land, if it pleafes him who deter-mines all things, that fhould be the cafe again.

I have this inftant learnt that we fet off to-morrow for Gravefend, where the fhip is laying, ready to fail; fhould we put into any port in the channel, I may probably write you if I am able, but muft now bid you adieu.

LETTER

LETTER II.

My dear Friend,

CONTRARY winds prevented us from proceeding directly out of the Channel, and made it neceſſary to put into this place. We have been here two days, but I am told there is an appearance of the wind changing, and that it is probable we ſhall make the attempt to get away ſome time this day; therefore I think it beſt not to defer performing my promiſe of writing to you, leaſt we fail, and I am diſappointed.

We embarked at Graveſend between eleven and twelve o'clock, the night after I wrote you. Every thing ſeemed in dreadful confuſion; but this I underſtand is commonly the caſe on board ſhips when on the eve of ſailing: beſides the captain had ſeveral friends who came from London to bid him farewell.

You

You may guefs that my mind, in fpite
of all the refolution a young girl is capable of muftering, could not be undif-
turbed; but I would not give way to any
melancholy reflections, and endeavoured
to fmother them as often as they intruded;
although I muft confefs they fometimes
caught me off my guard, and my heart
for the moment was ready to burft with
the thoughts of what I had to encounter,
which was pictured to me by almoft every
one in the worft of colours.

However I went to bed, and being
much fatigued, was in hopes every care
would be buried for the night in delightful fleep; but in this I was difappointed, for although my eyes were clofed
as foon as I got my head on the pillow,
yet it was not of long continuance.

I had flept perhaps two hours, when
the fhocking cries of murder awoke me:
I did not at the inftant recollect where I
was, but the firft thoughts which occurred
upon remembering myfelf on fhip-board
were, that a gang of pirates had attacked
the fhip, and would put us all to death.

All the cabin was by this time alarmed;
the cries of murder ftill continuing
while

while the captain and others were loudly calling for lights; and fo great was the confufion, that it was a long while before any could be procured: at length the light came, when I found myfelf fome what collected, and had courage enough to afk what was the matter.

My fears were removed, by being informed it was a Mr. B——, a paffenger, whofe intellects were a little deranged: he continued his difagreeable hideous cries the whole night, and prevented every one from fleeping ; for my part I fcarcely clofed my eyes again.

At breakfaft Mr. B—— apologized, by telling us that his wife had murdered his only child, for which reafon he had left her. " And," faid he, " the horrid act! has made fuch an impreffion on my mind, that I frequently think I fee her all befmeared with blood, with a dagger in her hand, determined to take away my life alfo : it preys upon my fpirits, for I want ftrength of mind to conquer the weaknefs."*

Mr.

---

* I am inclined to think this was only the imagination of a frantic brain, for we were not able to learn any thing more of the ftory.

Mr. Alexander Anderſon came on board, and dined: he politely enquired if I was comfortable; aſſured me, that every thing had been put on board to render us as much ſo as poſſible.

In the evening he returned to town, and we got under weigh.

Nothing occurred on our paſſage here except ſuch frequent returns of Mr. B's delirium, as has induced Captain Mc Lean to put him on ſhore, from the opinion of his being an unfit ſubjeƈt to go to the coaſt of Africa.

I did not experience any of thoſe fears peculiar to my ſex upon the water; and the only inconvenience I found was a little ſea ſickneſs, which I had a right to expeƈt, for you know this is my firſt voyage.

There is one circumſtance, which I forbode will make the remainder of our voyage unpleaſant.

The gentlemen whom Mr. Falcon-bridge is employed by are for aboliſh-ing the ſlave trade: the owners of this veſſel are of that trade, and conſequently
the

the Captain and Mr. Falconbridge muft
be very oppofite in their fentiments.

They are always arguing, and both
are warm in their tempers, which makes
me uneafy, and induces me to form the
conjectures I do; but perhaps that may
not be the cafe.

I have not been on fhore at Portfmouth, indeed it is not a defirable place
to vifit : I was once there, and few people have a wifh to fee it a fecond time.

The only thing that has attracted my
notice in the harbour, is the fleet with
the convicts for Botany Bay, which are
wind bound, as well as ourfelves.

The deftiny of fuch numbers of my
fellow creatures has made what I expect
to encounter, fet lighter upon my mind
than it ever did before ; nay, nothing
could have operated a reconciliation fo
effectually ; for as the human heart is
more fufceptible of diftrefs conveyed
by the eye, than when reprefented by
language however ingenuoufly pictured
with mifery, fo the fight of thofe unfortunate beings, and the thoughts of
what they are to endure, have worked
more forcibly on my feelings than all
the

the accounts I ever read or heard of wretchednefs before.

I muft clofe this which is the laft, in all probability, you will receive from me, 'till my arrival in Africa; when, if an opportunity offers, I fhall make a point of writing to you.

Pray do not let diftance or abfence blot out the recollection of her,

Who is truly your's.

LETTER

LETTER III.

BANCE ISLAND, *Feb.* 10, 1791

My dear Friend,

WE failed the very day I wrote you from Portfmouth, and our paffage was unufually quick, being only eighteen days from thence to this place.

The novelty of a fhip ploughing the tracklefs ocean, in a few days became quite familiar to me; there was fuch a famenefs in every thing (for fome birds were all we faw the whole way) that I found the voyage tirefome, notwithftanding the fhortnefs of it.

You will readily believe my heart was gladdened at the fight of the mountains of Sierra Leone, which was the land we firft made.

Thofe mountains appear to rife gradually from the fea to a ftupendous height, richly wooded and beautifully ornamented
by

by the hand of nature, with a variety of delightful profpects.

I was vaftly pleafed while failing up the river, for the rapidity of the fhip through the water afforded a courfe of new fcenery almoft every moment, till we caft anchor here: Now and then I faw the glimpfe of a native town, but from the diftance and new objects haftily catching my eye, was not able to form a judgment or idea of any of them; but this will be no lofs, as I may have frequent opportunities of vifiting fome of them hereafter.

As foon as our anchor was dropped, Captain Mc Lean faluted Bance Ifland with feven guns, which not being returned I enquired the caufe, and was told that the laft time the Duke of Buccleugh came out, fhe, as is cuftomary, faluted, and on the fort returning the compliment, a wad was drove by the force of the fea breeze upon the roof of one of the houfes (which was then of thatch) fet fire to the building, and confumed not only the houfe but goods to a large amount.

When the ceremony of faluting was over, Captain Mc Lean and Mr. W. Falconbridge

conbridge went on fhore; but it being late in the evening, I continued on board 'till next day.

Here we met the Lapwing cutter. She failed fome time before us from Europe, and had been arrived two or three weeks.

The mafter of her, and feveral of the people to whofe affiftance Mr. Falconbridge is come, and who had taken refuge here, came to vifit us.

They reprefented their fufferings to have been very great; that they had been treacheroufly dealt with by one *King* Jemmy, who had drove them away from the ground they occupied, burnt their houfes, and otherwife devefted them of every comfort and neceffary of life; they alfo threw out fome reflections againft the Agent of this ifland; faid he had fold feveral of their fellow fufferers to a Frenchman, who had taken them to the Weft Indies.

Mr. Falconbridge, however, was not the leaft inclined to give entire confidence to what they told us; but prudently fufpended his opinion until he had made further enquiries.

Thofe

Thofe vifitors being gone, we retired to bed—I cannot fay to reft; the heat was fo exceffive that I fcarcely flept at all.

The following day we received a polite invitation to dine on fhore, which I did not objeЕ to, although haraffed for want of fleep the night before.

At dinner the converfation turned upon the flave trade: Mr. Falconbridge, zealous for the caufe in which he is engaged, ftrenuoufly oppofed every argument his opponents advanced in favour of the *abominable* trade: the glafs went brifkly round, and the gentlemen growing warm, I retired immediately as the cloath was removed.

The people on the ifland crowded to fee me; they gazed with apparent aftonifhment—I fuppofe at my drefs, for white women could not be a novelty to them, as there were feveral among the unhappy people fent out here by government, one of whom is now upon the ifland.

Seeing fo many of my own fex, though of different complexions from myfelf, attired in their native garbs, was a fcene
equally

equally new to me, and my delicacy, I confefs, was not a little hurt at times.

Many among them appeared of fu-perior rank, at leaft I concluded fo from the preferable way in which they were clad; nor was I wrong in my conjeƈture, for upon enquiring who they were, was informed one was the *woman* or *miſtreſs* of Mr. — —, another of Mr. B——, and fo on: I then underſtood that every gen-tleman on the iſland had his *lady*.

While I was thus entertaining myſelf with my new acquaintances, two or three of the gentlemen left their wine and joined me; among them was Mr. B——, the agent; he in a very friendly manner begged I would take a bed on ſhore.

I thanked him, and ſaid, if agreeable to Mr. Falconbridge, I would have no objeƈtion: however, Falconbridge ob-jeƈted, and gave me for reafon that he had been unhandſomely treated, and was determined to go on board the Lapwing, for he would not ſubjeƈt himſelf to any obligation to men poſſeſſing ſuch *diabo-lical* ſentiments.

It was not proper for me to contradict him at this moment, as the heat of
argument and the influence of an over
portion of wine had *quickened* and *dis-*
concerted his temper; I therefore fub-
mitted without making any objection to
come on board this tub of a veffel, which
in point of fize and cleanlinefs, comes
nigher a hog-trough than any thing elfe
you can imagine.

Though I refolved to remonftrate the
firft feafonable opportunity, and to point
out the likelihood of endangering my
health, fhould he perfift to keep me in
fo confined a place.

This remonftrance I made the next
morning, after paffing a night of torment,
but to no purpofe; the only confolation
I got was,—as foon as the fettlers could
be collected, he would have a houfe built
on fhore, where they were to be fixed.

I honeftly own my original refolutions
of firmnefs was now warped at what I
forefaw I was doomed to fuffer, by being imprifoned, for God knows how long,
in a place fo difgufting as this was, in
my opinion, at that time.

Conceive

Conceive yourfelf pent up in a floating cage, without room either to walk about, ftand erect, or even to lay at length; expofed to the inclemency of the weather, having your eyes and ears momently offended by acts of indecency, and language too horrible to relate—add to this a complication of filth, the ftench from which was continually affailing your nofe, and then you will have a faint notion of the Lapwing Cutter.

However, upon collecting myfelf, and recollecting there was no remedy but to make the beft of my fituation, I begged the mafter (who flept upon deck in confequence of my coming on board) to have the cabin thoroughly cleaned and wafhed with vinegar; intreated Falconbridge to let me go on fhore while it was doing, and hinted at the indecencies I faw and heard, and was promifed they would be prevented in future.

With thefe affurances I went on fhore, not a little elated at the reprieve I was to enjoy for a few hours.

The gentlemen received me with every mark of attention and civility; indeed, I muft be wanting in fenfibility, if my heart

did

did not warm with gratitude to Meffrs. Ballingall and Tilly, for their kindneffes to me: the latter gentleman I am informed will fucceed to the agency of the ifland; he is a genteel young man, and I am told, very defervedly, a favourite with his employers.

Mr. Falconbridge this day fent a meffage to Elliotte Griffiths, the fecretary of Naimbana, who is the King of Sierra Leone, acquainting him with the purport of his miffion, and begging to know when he may be honored with an audience of *his Majesty.*

In the evening he received an anfwer, of which the following is a copy :

Robana Town.

KING Naimbana's compliments to Mr. Falconbridge, and will be glad to fee him to-morrow.

(Signed)

A. E. Griffiths, Sec.

Such an immediate anfwer from a *King*, I confidered a favorable omen, and a mark
of

of condefcenfion in his Majefty, but the
refult you fhall hear by and by; in the
mean while, I muft tell you what paffed
the remainder of the day at Bance Ifland,
and give, as far as my ideas will allow me,
a defcription of this factory.

We fat down to dinner with the fame
party as the firft day, confifting of about
fifteen in number; this neceffary ceremony
ended, and towards the cool of the afternoon, I propofed walking for a while:
Mr. Tilly and a Mr. Barber offered to
accompany and fhow me the ifland, which
not being objected to, we fet out.

Adam's Town was the firft place they
took me to; it is fo called from a native
of that name, who has the management
of all the gramattos, or free black fervants,
but under the control of the Agent.

The whole town confifts of a ftreet with
about twenty-five houfes on each fide:—
on the right of all is Adam's houfe.

This building does not differ from the
reft, except in fize, being much more
fpacious than any other, and being bar-
racaded

racaded with a mud wall;—all of them
are compofed of thatch, wood, and clay,
fomething refembling our poor cottages,
in many parts of England.

I went into feveral of them—faw nothing that did not difcover the occupiers
to be very clean and neat; in fome was
a block or two of wood, which ferved for
chairs,—a few wooden bowls or trenchers,
and perhaps a pewter bafon and an iron
pot, compleated the whole of their furniture.

In every houfe I was accofted by who-
ever we found at home, in the Timmany
language *Currea Yaa*, which fignifies——
How do you do, mother ? — the moft
refpeɛtful way they can addrefs any perfon.

Leaving the town, we proceeded firft
to the burying ground for Europeans,
and then to that for the blacks ; — the
only diftinɛtion between them was a few
orange trees, that fhaded two grave-
ftones at the former,—one in memory
of a Mr. Knight, who had died here
after refiding fifteen years as Agent;—
the other on the fuppofed grave of a
Captain Tittle, who was murdered by
one Signior Domingo, a native chief, for
(as

(as Domingo afferts) being the caufe of his fon's death.

The circumftance leading to the murder, and of the murder itfelf, has been reprefented to me nearly in the following words:

" One day while the fon of Domingo was employed by Captain Tittle, as a gramatto, or pull away boy,* Tittle's hat by accident blew overboard, and he infifted that the boy fhould jump into the water and fwim after it, as the only means of faving his hat.

" The boy obftinately refufed, faying, he could not fwim, and he fhould either be drowned, or the fharks would catch him; upon which Tittle pufhed him into the water, and the poor boy was loft; but whether devoured by fharks, or fuffocated by water, is immaterial, he was never heard of, or feen after.

" The father, though forely grieved for his fon's death, was willing to confider it as accidental, and requefted Tittle would fupply him with a fmall quantity of rum to make a cry or lamentation in their country cuftom.

The

* African term for an Oar-man.

" The Captain, by promife, acquiefced to the demand, and fent him a cafk ; but, inftead of Spirit, filled with emptyings from the *tubs* of his flaves.

" As foon as Domingo difcovered this infult and impofition, he informed Tittle he muft either fubmit to the decifion of a Palaver, or he would put him to death if ever an opportunity offered ; but Tittle laughed at thefe threats, and difregarded them, vauntingly threw himfelf into the way of Domingo—while the trick played upon him, and the lofs of his fon were frefh in his memory.

" The African, however, inftead of being daunted at the fight of this head-ftrong man, foon convinced him he was ferious : he had Tittle feized, and after confining him fome time in irons, with-out food, ordered him to be broken to death, which was executed under the in-fpeftion of the injured father, and to the great joy and fatisfaftion of a multitude of fpeftators."

Not a fentence or hint of the affair is mentioned on the tombftone ; the reafon affigned for the omiffion, was a wifh to obliterate the melancholy cataftrophe, and a

fear

fear left the record might be the means of kindling animofities at a future day.

Now, although I cannot without hor-ror contemplate on the untimely end of this man, yet he affuredly in fome de-gree merited it, if the account I have heard, and juft now related to you, be true, which I have no reafon to queftion ; for he who unprovoked can wantonly rob a fellow creature of his life, deferves not life himfelf !

From the catacombs which lay at the fouth eaft end, we walked to the oppofite point of the ifland ; it is no great diftance, for the whole ifland is very little more than a fourth of a mile in length, and fcarcely a mile and a half in circumference.

Several rocks lay at a fmall diftance from the fhore at this end; they are by the natives called the Devil's Rocks,— from a fuperftitious opinion, that the *old Gentleman* refides either there or in the neighbourhood.

Sammo, King of the Bulloms, comes to this place once a year to make a facrifice and peace-offering to his Infernal Majefty.

From

From this King Meffrs. Anderfons hold all their poffeffions here, and I underftand they pay him an annual tribute—but to what amount I cannot fay.

The King comes in perfon to receive his dues, which are paid him in his canoe, for he never ventures to put his foot on fhore, as his *Gree Greemen* or fortune-tellers have perfuaded him the ifland will fink under him, if ever he lands.

I am told at one time he fuffered himfelf to be dragged up to the Factory Houfe in his boat, but no argument was ftrong enough to feduce him to difembark, for he did not confider he incurred the penalty his prophets denounced while he continued in his canoe; though he could not avoid fhewing evident tokens of uneafinefs, till he was fafe afloat again.

We now returned to the Factory, or as it is otherwife called Bance Ifland Houfe.

This building at a diftance has a re-fpectable and formidable appearance; nor is it much lefs fo upon a nearer invefti-gation: I fuppofe it is about one hun-dred feet in length, and thirty in breadth, and

and contains nine rooms, on one floor, under which are commodious large cellars and ftore rooms; to the right is the kitchen, forge, &c. and to the left other neceffary buildings, all of country ftone, and furrounded with a prodigious thick lofty wall.

There was formerly a fortification in front of thofe houfes, which was deftroyed by a French frigate during the laft war; at prefent feveral pieces of cannon are planted in the fame place, but without embrafures or breaft-work; behind the great houfe is the flave yard, and houfes for accommodating the flaves.

Delicacy, perhaps, prevented the gentlemen from taking me to fee them; but the room where we dined looks directly into the yard.

Involuntarily I ftrolled to one of the windows a little before dinner, without the fmalleft fufpicion of what I was to fee;— judge then what my aftonifhment and feelings were, at the fight of between two and three hundred wretched victims, chained and parcelled out in circles, juft fatisfying the cravings of nature from a trough of rice placed in the centre of each circle.

Offended

Offended modefty rebuked me with a blufh for not hurrying my eyes from fuch difgufting fcenes; but whether fafcinated by female curiofity, or whatever elfe, I could not withdraw myfelf for feveral minutes—while I remarked fome whofe hair was withering with age, reluctantly tafting their food — and others thoughtlefs from youth, greedily deouring all before them; be affured I avoided the profpects from this fide of the houfe ever after.

Having prolonged the time till nine at night, we returned to our floating prifon, and what with the affiduity of the mafter in removing many inconveniencies, my mind being more at eafe, want of reft for two nights, and fomewhat fatigued with the exercife of the day, I thank God, flept charmingly, and the next morning we fet fail for Robana, where we arrived about ten o'clock: I think it is called nine miles from Bance Ifland.

We went on fhore, and rather caught his *Majesty* by furprife, for he was quite in *dishabille;* and at our approach retired in great hafte.

I ob-

I obferved a perfon pafs me in a loofe white frock and trowfers, *whom I would not have suspected for a King!* if he had not been pointed out to me.

Mr. Elliotte and the *Queen* met us; and after introducing her Majefty and himfelf, we were then conducted to her houfe.

She behaved with much indifference,— told me, in broken Englifh, the *King* would come prefently,—he was gone to *pegininee* woman houfe to drefs himfelf.

After fetting nigh half an hour, Naimbana made his appearance, and received us with feeming good will: he was dreffed in a purple embroidered coat, white fattin waiftcoat and breeches, *thread stockings*, and his left fide emblazoned with a flaming ftar; his legs to be fure were *harliquined*, by a number of holes in the ftockings, through which his black fkin appeared.

Compliments ended, Mr. Falconbridge acquainted him with his errand, by a repetition of what he wrote the day before: and complained much of King Jemmy's injuftice, in driving the fettlers away, and burning their town.

The

The King anfwered through Elliotte,
(for he fpeaks but little Englifh) that
Jemmy was partly right—the people had
brought it on themfelves; they had taken
part with fome Americans, with whom
Jemmy had a difpute, and through that
means drew the ill will of this man upon
them, who had behaved, confidering their
conduct, as well as they merited; for he
gave them three days notice before he
burned their town, that they might remove
themfelves and all their effects away;
that he (Naimbana) could not prudently
re-eftablifh them, except by confent of all
the Chiefs—for which purpofe he muft
call a court or palaver; but it would be
feven or eight days before they could be
collected; however he would fend a fummons to the different parties directly, and
give Falconbridge timely advice when they
were to meet.

Falconbridge perceived clearly nothing
was to be effected without a palaver, and
unlefs the King's intereft was fecured his
views would be fruftrated, and his endeavours ineffectual; but how this was to be
done, or what expedient to adopt, he was
at a lofs for.

He

He confidered it impolitic to purchafe
his patronage by heavy prefents, leaft
the other great men might expeƈt the
fame; and he had it not in his power to
purchafe them all in the fame way, as the
fcanty cargo of the Lapwing would not
admit of it.

At length, trufting that the praife-worthy
purpofes he was aiming at infured him the
affiftance of the King of Kings he refolved to try what good words would do.

Having prefaced his arguments with a
fmall donation of rum, wine, cheefe, and
a gold laced hat, (which Naimbana feemed
much pleafed with) Falconbridge began,
by explaining what advantages would ac-
crue to his *Majesty*, and to all the inhabitants round about, by fuch an eftablifhment as the St. George's Bay Company were defirous of making ;——the
good they wifhed to do—*their disinterested-
ness in point of obtaining wealth*, and concluded by expoftulating on the injuftice
and impofition of difpoffeffing the late fettlers of the grounds and houfes they occupied, which had been honeftly and
honorably purchafed by Captain Thompfon
of

of the Navy, in the name of our gracious Sovereign, his Britannic Majesty.

That it was unusual for Englishmen to forego fulfilling any engagements they made ; and they held in detestation every person so disposed.

He then entreated the King would use all his might to prevent any unfavourable prejudices which a refusal to reinstate the Settlers, or to confirm the bargain made with Captain Thompson, might operate against him in the minds of his good friends the King of England and the St. George's Bay Company.

The King said he liked the English in preference to all white men, tho' he considered every white man as a *rogue*, and consequently saw them with a jealous eye; yet, he believed the English were by far the honestest, and for that reason, notwithstanding he had received more favors from the French than the English, he liked the latter much best.

He was decidedly of opinion, that all contracts or agreements between man and man however disadvantageous to either party should be binding; but observed,

he

he was *hastily drawn in* to difpofe of land
to Captain Thompfon, *which in fact he had
not a right to fell,* becaufe fays he, " this
is a great country, and belongs to many
people—where I live belongs to myfelf—
and I can live where I like; nay, can
appropriate any unhabited land within my
dominions to what ufe I pleafe; but it is
neceffary for me to obtain the confent of
my people, or rather the head man of
every town, before I fell any land to a
white man, or allow ftrangers to come
and live among us."

" *I should have done this you will say at
first*—Granted—but as I difobliged my
fubjects by fuffering your people to take
poffeffion of the land without their appro-
bation, from which caufe I was not able
to protect them, unlefs I hazarded civil
commotions in my country; and as they
have been *turned away*—it is beft now—
they fhould be replaced by the unanimous
voice of all interefted.

" I am bound from what I have heretofore done, to give my utmoft fupport;
and if my people do not acquiefce, it fhall
not be my fault."

Here

Here Falconbrigde, interrupting the King, faid—" The King of the Englifh will not blame your people, but load yourfelf with the ftigma; it is King *Naimbana* who is oftenfible to King *George*—and I hope King, you will not fall out with your good friend."

This being explained by *Mr. Secretary Elliotte*, his Majefty was fome moments filent—when clafping Falconbridge in his arms, told him—" *I believe you and King George* are my good friends—do not fear, have a good heart, I will do as much as I can for you."

They then fhook hands heartily, and Naimbana retired, I fuppofe to his *Pegininee woman's house*, but prefently returned dreffed in a fuit of black velvet, except the ftockings, which were the fame as before.

I often had an inclination to offer my fervices to clofe the holes: but was fearful leaft my needle might blunder into his *Majesty*'s leg, and ftart the blood, for drawing the blood of an African King, I am informed, whether occafioned by accident or otherwife, is punifhed with death;

death: the dread of this only prevented me.

We were now invited to walk and fee the town, while dinner was preparing.

It confifts of about twenty houfes ir-regularly placed, built of the fame ma-terials, but in a fuperior way to thofe of Adam's town; — the whole of them are either occupied by the King's wives and fervants, or appropriated as warehoufes.

I faw feveral of his wives, but his *Pe-gininee* woman is a moft beautiful young girl of about fourteen.

None of them are titled with the ap-pellation of *Queen*, but the oldeft, who I was introduced to, and by whom the King has feveral children; one of the daughter's, named Clara, is wife to El-liotte, and a fon named Bartholomew, is now in France for his education.

In different parts of the town I obferved fome rags ftuck on poles, at the foot of each were placed—perhaps a rufty cutlafs, fome pieces of broken glafs, and a pew-ter bafon, containing a liquid of fome fort;

fort ; thefe are called *Gree Grees*, and confidered as antidotes againft the Devil's
vengeance.

I was thoughtlefsly offering to examine
one of them, when Mr. Elliotte requefted me to defift, or I fhould give
offence, they being held in a very fa-
cred point of view.

We were now led to the garden,
which was only furnifhed with African
plants, fuch as pines, melons, pumpkins,
cucumbers, &c. &c.

The King cut two beautiful pines and
prefented to me : he then fhewed us a
large new houfe, at prefent building for
him, which is after the fame form, and
of the fame materials with the reft of his
town, but much larger.

In our walk we faw many of the
King's flaves employed in preparing the
palm-nut, to make oil from them : It may
not be amifs here .to give you fome defcription of the tree which produce thefe
nuts.

It is remarkable ſtrait and of a gigantic height; the trunk is quite naked, having neither limb or bark, for the only branches grow immediately from the top, and incline their points ſomewhat towards the ground.

This is a valuable tree, the nut not only produces a quantity of oil, but is eſteemed excellent food by the natives, who alſo extract a liquor from the tree, which they call palm wine.

This I am told is done by means of an inciſion in the upper part of the trunk, in which a pipe is entered to to convey the liquor into bottles placed beneath.

I have taſted ſome of this wine, and do not think it unpleaſant when freſh made; it has a ſweetiſh taſte, and much the look of whey, but foments in a few days, and grows four—however I really think this liquor diſtilled would make a decent kind of ſpirit.

Having ſeen all the raree-ſhows of Robana town, we returned to the Queens houſe to dinner, which was ſhortly after put on a table covered with a plain
calico

calico cloth, and confifted of boiled and broiled fowls, rice, and fome greens re-fembling our fpinnage.

But I fhould tell you, before dinner Naimbana again changed his drefs for a fcarlet robe embroidered with gold.

Naimbana, Elliotte, Falconbridge, and myfelf, only fet down; the Queen ftood behind the King eating an onion I gave her, a bite of which fhe now and then indulged her *Royal Confort* with: filver forks were placed on the King's plate, and mine, but no where elfe.

The King is rather above common height, but meagre withal; the features of his face refemble a European more than any black I have feen; his teeth are moftly decayed, and his hair, or rather wool, befpeaks old age, which I judge to be about eighty; he was feldom without a fmile on his countenance, but I think his fmiles were fufpicious.

He gave great attention while Falcon-bridge was fpeaking, for though he does not fpeak our language, he underftands a good deal of it; his anfwers were flow, and on the whole tolerably reafonable.

The

The Queen is of a middle ſtature, plump and jolly; her temper ſeems placid and accommodating; her teeth are bad, but I dare ſay ſhe has otherwiſe been a good looking woman in her youthful days.

I ſuppoſe her now to be about forty-five or ſix, at which age women are con-ſidered old here.

She ſat on the King's right hand, while he and Falconbridge were in con-verſation; and now and then would clap her hands, and cry out *Ya hoo,* which ſignifies, that's well or proper.

She was dreſſed in the country man-ner, but in a dignified ſtile, having ſeve-ral yards of ſtriped taffety wrapped round her waiſt, which ſerved as a petticoat; another piece of the ſame was care-leſsly thrown over her ſhoulders in form of a ſcarf; her head was decorated with two ſilk handkerchiefs; her ears with rich gold ear-rings, and her neck with gaudy necklaces; *but she had neither shoes nor stockings on.*

Clara was dreſſed much after the ſame way, but her apparel was not quite of

fuch good materials as the Queen's : Mr.
Elliotte apologized after dinner, that for
want of *sugar* they could not offer tea
or coffee.

The tide ferving, and approaching
night obliged us to reimbark and return
to this place.

On the whole I was much pleafed
with the occurrences of the day ; indeed,
methinks, I hear you faying, " Why the
week mind of this giddy girl will be quite
intoxicated with the courtefy and attention paid her by fuch great folks ;" but
believe me, to whatever height of felf-
confequence I may have been lifted by
aerial fancies, overpouring fleep prevailed, and clouding all my greatnefs—
I awoke next morning without the flighest
remains of fancied importance.

The news of our arrival having by this
time circulated through different parts of
the country, we found feveral, who either
excited by curiofity or fome other caufe,
had come here to pay their obeifance, or
as the Africans term it, *make service* to us ;
but there was none of note or quality
worth naming among thofe vifitors, except
an elderly man called *Pa,* or *Father Boson,*
who

who is the head man of a confiderable
town about fifty miles up the river, and
who, guided by the impulfe of a good
heart, invited the wretched exiles in the
hour of diftrefs to refuge at his place,
which was excepted by the greater part,
who have been foftered and protected ever
fince by the almsdeeds of this good old
man; he was habited in a white linen
furplice, and a cap of the fame, and
made, I affure you a reverential appearance.

I am told this is the drefs of a nation
in the interior country, called Mundin-
goes; but **Pa Bofon** is not a Mundingo
himfelf.

He refpectfully accofted me in broken
Englifh, and bending his knee, offered
me his right hand fupported under the
elbow by his left.

I held out my hand which he flightly
touched, and then repeated the fame to
Falconbridge: he was now invited to be
feated under the awning we had erected
over the Lapwing's deck—when he detail-
ed a moft pitiable account of fufferings
and hardfhips which the unfortunate
people had undergone; but he faid
there were many bad people among
them,

them, who had abufed his kindnefs by
ingratitude.

Falconbridge and myfelf endeavoured
what we could to convince him we were
highly pleafed with his behaviour; but
as words are not fufficient to convey
thankful acknowledgments in this country, Falconbridge confirmed the affurances we made by a prefent of a
quantity of rum, and fome hard ware,
and a promife to reprefent his conduct
to the St. George's Bay Company, in a
proper light, which he was certain would
induce them to make a more ample re-
compence at a future time.

Well pleafed with his reception, and
fomewhat enebriated with the effects of
repeated glaffes of fpirits he had taken,
Pa Bofon left us; but firft promifing
faithfully he would befriend us all in his
power at the Palaver.

He travelled with much feeming confequence: his canoe was longer than our
cutter, and manned with fourteen people,
viz. ten oarsmen, a cockfwain, two poig
nard bearers, and another who beat time
on a flat founding drum to a fong given
out by the cockfwain, and re-echoed by
the

the oarsmen; the fong I am told was expreffive of praifes to their Chief, and of their fatisfaction for the treatment they had received from us.

The following day we vifited a fmall ifland named Taffo, oppofite to Bance ifland, at about one mile and a half diftance.

This is a well wooded ifland and I fhould fuppofe if cultivated would be a fruitful one.*

It fupplies Bance ifland with water, which is remarkable fine, and the prefent holders of the latter claim a right to this alfo, but upon what grounds I cannot fay.

Approaching the fhore I faw many monkies playing on the beach and catching fmall fifh at the edge of the water, but they all ran away as we drew near; being informed there was no danger to be apprehended from wild beafts of prey, we penetrated fome diftance into the woods.

In

---

* A fmall part of this ifland is now planted with cotton, coffee, and fugar cane, for account of Meffrs. Anderfons.

In our walk we faw many pine apples
and lime trees, the fpontaneous produc-
tion of the country, and a variety of birds
beautifully plumed, but none that fung.

We were alfo treated with the perfumes
of fragrant aromatic plants, and indeed
were vaftly delighted and entertained,
though I felt fatigued, with our per-
ambulation.

The next day, we went up the river,
about twelve miles, to fee a fecret or
referved factory belonging to Bance Ifland
at a place called Marre Bump, but our
curiofity had nearly led us into a ferious
fcrape.

Falconbridge neglected to obtain permiffion, and confequently had no fanc-
tion, from the Proprietors.

After landing we walked, at leaft half
a mile on a narrow path, through amazing
thick woods before we reached the houfes;
as foon as the inhabitants perceived us,
the women took to their heels and ran to
the woods, the men flew to arms, and in a
moment we were met by more than twenty
huge fellows armed with guns, piftols and
cutlaffes.

We

We were four in number, viz. Falconbridge, the mafter of the cutter, a Black man and myfelf; our Black fpoke to them in their own language—they would not liften to him; but faid, if we did not return immediately the way we came, they would put us all to death.

It is eafier for you to imagine what horrors thofe threats occafioned, than for me to point them out.

Finding argument fruitlefs, we put to the right about, and haftened to our boat; they, following, flanked us on each fide of the road, watchfully obferving our motions till they faw us clear off, when, as a mark of exultation, they difcharged their mufkets over our heads, and made the woods ring with peals of triumphant clamor.

Recovering from my fright a little, I could not help, you may fuppofe, exulting (though in a different way) as well as the favages.

My heart overflowed with gratitude, to the Author of its animation, for our providential efcape.

Returning

Returning down the river, we obferved numbers of orange trees, a clufter of them, overloaded with fruit, invited us on fhore, and after gathering what we chofe, made the beft of our way, and arrived here before night.

Three days are now elapfed fince our expedition to Marre Bump, during which time I have confined myfelf moftly on board, occupied in writing this letter.

It has been, really, a fatiguing job, being obliged to fit in bed with a book placed on my knee, which ferves for a writing defk; but I was determined whatever the inconveniencies might be, not to let flip an opportunity, as I find they but feldom offer.

I lament the Palaver is not over, that I might give you my account of an African Court, but my next will remedy this lofs.

Mr. Elliotte has informed us the Chiefs will be at Robana the day after to-morrow, when Falconbridge is defired to attend; I fhall accompany him, and long to know the refult.

Adieu, Heaven blefs you, &c. &c.

LETTER

LETTER III.

GRANVILLE TOWN, SIERRA LEONE.
May 13, 1791.

My dear Friend,

OCCASIONAL vifits to Bance Ifland, unattended by any important Occurrence worth troubling you with, and a continual concourfe of ftrangers, making their African compliments, en-groffed two days interval between the date of my laft letter, and our fecond expedition to Robana; when we fet out in a boat and four hands, taking with us plenty of fpirits for the common people, and a little wine for the King and his affociates.

When we came in fight of the Town, Multitudes of people thronged to the Beach.

Mr. Elliotte met us at the boat, and the croud formed an avenue, through which

which he conducted us to the Queen's houfe, amidft fuch thundering accla- mations, that it was almoft impoffible to hear one or other fpeak.

The King and Queen met us at the door, and feemed to give us a hearty welcome.

We were then ufhered in, and intro- duced in general terms to the company, confifting of the parties who were to compofe the Court, (and a multiplicity of women,) their wives, daughters, and attendants.

Having feated ourfelves, and wafted almoft an hour in receiving the civilities of fhaking hands with every individual in the room, the members of the Court then took their feats, round the large table we dined off, when firft there ; which was now covered with a green cloth.

The King fat at the head of the table in an old arm chair : on his right was his fecretary, and on his left his Palavar man ; or, as the office is termed in England, his Attorney general : the other Chiefs appeared to feat themfelves by feniority ;

feniority; the oldeft next the *Throne*, if I may fo term the *old chair.*

The King wore his hat, which was the gold laced one Falconbridge gave him.

On the table was placed wine and rum, of which every one helped himfelf plentifully.

I was aftonifhed to fee, not only the men, but women drink rum in half pints at a time, as deliberately as I would water.

After amufing themfelves fome time in this way, Mr. Palaver Man got up, bending his right knee, prefented his *Majesty* with fome Cola* from the crown of his hat, then retired to the oppofite end of the table, when he opened the bufinefs of the day, by a fpeech of at leaft an hour and a half long; it being in their own language, I, of courfe, did not underftand a word, but during the

* A fruit much efteemed in Africa, not unlike a horfe chefnut, but fomewhat larger. It is an excellent bitter.

the time he fpoke, there was the greateft
filence and attention obferved.

The next fpokefman, was King Jemmy,
who previoufly went through the fame ceremony his predeceffor had done : whether
this man's language was eloquent or not,
I cannot be a judge, but his vociferation
was enough to deafen one; though I had
reafon to think what he faid gave great
fatisfaction to the by-ftanders, who frequently interrupted him by clapping of
hands and fhouts of, *Ya Hoo ! Ya Hoo!
Ya Hoo !* and other tokens of applaufe.

My heart quivered with fear leaft they
might be forming fome treacherous contrivance : I could not conceal the uneafinefs it felt : My countenance betrayed me,
a fhower of tears burft from my eyes, and
I fwooned into hyftericks.

Recovering in a fhort time, I obferved
every one around, treating me with the
utmoft kindnefs, and endeavouring to
convince me that neither infult or injury would be offered us : but my fears
were not to be removed, or even
checked haftily, for I had fcarcely got
the better of my fright at Marre Bump;
however

however I ftruggled to awaken my refolution, and collected enough, after awhile,
to affect compofure; but believe me it
was mere affectation: Night was drawing
nigh, and I folicited Falconbridge to return as foon as poffible: He argued, the
Court had been impeded by the aukward
fituation my fears had thrown me into: but
he would fet out time enough to reach
Bance Island before dark.

The Affembly now refumed their bufinefs.

One or two members offered Cola to
the King, which he refufed; a grey head-
ed old man then made the offer, and
it being accepted, he took the foot of the
table, and a few words compleating
what he had to fay: Mr. Elliotte intimated
that King Naimbana intended to give
his fentiments; upon which every member rofe up, and the King continuing
in his chair, covered, delivered his fpeech
in a concife, clear, and refpectable manner.

After this Mr. Elliotte acquainted
Falconbridge the Court could not come
to one mind that night, but it was
generally

generally underſtood, if he would give
fifteen hundred Bars,* they would confirm King Naimbana's engagement with
Captain Thompſon, and re-eſtabliſh his
people.

Falconbridge, whom you know is naturally of an irritable diſpoſition, quickened
at Elliotte's information; but had prudence
enough only to ſay, he ſhould conſider
ſuch a demand very extravagant, and
his ſmall cargo, which he was deſired to
appropriate another way, would not permit him to pay ſo much, if he had the
inclination.

We then made our congees, and
took leave of thoſe African *gentry* ; indeed it was high time, for the liquor
they had drank began to operate powerfully : Mr. Elliotte and ſeveral others
accompanied us to the boat: in our
walk thither, he much admired a handſome fowling piece of Mr. Falconbridge's,
which

* A Bar is the nominal price of a certain quantity of goods, which the natives formerly conſider-
ed of equal value with a bar of iron ; but at preſent
they do not appear to have any criterion : two
pounds of tobacco is a bar, and two yards of fine
India cotton, or a yard of rich ſilk is no more.

which Falconbridge without hefitation re
quefted he would accept. thinking fuçh an
immediate fhew of generofity might have
a favourable tendency.

Both of us promifed to be down again
the following day, when it was expected
the Palavar would be finifhed: but I
muft be honeft and tell you, I was refolved not to vifit Robana again, while
this mock judicatory lafted.

About feven o'clock we reached the
Cutter; I was almoft famifhed with want
of food, for I had not eat a morfel the
whole day: there was not a thing on
board, but falt beef, fo hard, we were
obliged to chop it with an axe, and
fome mouldy, rotten bifcuits; however, fo great was my hunger, that I
could not help fatisfying it with fome
of this beef and bread, uncouth as it
was.

In the morning I feigned ficknefs,
and beg'd to be excufed from attending Falconbridge; he therefore fet out,
reluctantly leaving me behind: when
he was gone, I went on fhore, and
fpent the day in comfort and pleafantry, under the hofpitable roof of Bance
Ifland

Ifland houfe; where I related the adventures of the preceding day, which afforded much mirth and glee to the company.

I met one Rennieu (a Frenchman) there; he has a factory at a fmall Ifland, called Gambia, up another branch of this River, named Bunch River, whither he politely invited me, and made a tender of any thing in his power to ferve us.

Before Falconbridge returned, which was not till between eight and nine o'clock at night, I had not only got on board, but in bed, and as he did not afk how I had fpent the day, I did not inform him: he was vexed and out of humor, faid he thought the wretches were only *bamboozl ng* him, he believed they would do nothing but drink the liquor, while he had a drop to carry them, for he was no forwarder than the day before.

In this manner he was obliged to repeat his vifits for five fucceffive days, before he got their final decifion, which however, was at laft tolerably favorable on our fide.

They

They confented to re-eftablifh the people, and to grant to the St. George's Bay Company, all the land King Naimbana had formerly fold Captain Thompfon; for a paltry confideration, of about thirty pounds; and for the good faith and true performance of the contraft, the King faid he would pledge his fecond fon John Frederic, whom Falconbridge might take with him to England : In anfwer to this offer, Falconbridge told Naimbana, he would be very glad to take his fon to England, where he was fure the Company would have him educated and treated kindly without confidering him a hoftage.

This pleafed the old man vaftly, and it was agreed, John Frederic fhall accompany us, when we leave Africa.

The following or fixth day, Falconbridge had engaged to carry down to Robana the ftipulated goods for repurchafing the land, and by his importunities, I was prevailed on to accompany him. We arrived early in the morning, and having foon made a delivery of the goods, which was all the bufinefs for the day, I was juk about expreffing a defire to fee fome falt works,
I learned

I learned were upon the Ifland, when the King, as though he had anticipated my wifhes, enquired if we liked to fee them ? if fo, he would walk there with us : We accordingly went, paffing in our way a hamlet or two, inhabited by the King's flaves.

Thefe works lay near a mile from the town, and are a parcel of fmall holes, or bafons formed in a low, muddy place ; they are fupplied with fea water, which the burning fun quickly exhales, leaving the faline particles, and by frequent repetition, a quantity of falt is thus accumulated, which the King conveys into, and difpofes of in the interior country, for flaves.

Making this falt is attended with a very trifling expence, for none but *old, refuse, female* flaves, are employed in the work, and the profit is confiderable.

Early in the afternoon we returned to Bance Ifland, taking Clara, the wife of Elliotte, with us : She remained with me feveral days, during which I had opportunities (for I made a point of it) to try her difpofition ; I found it impetuous, litigious, and implacable : I endeavoured

deavoured to perfuade her to drefs in the European way, but to no purpofe; fhe would tear the clothes off her back immediately after I put them on.

Finding no credit could be gained by trying to new fafhion this *Ethiopian* Prin-cefs, I got rid of her as foon as poffible.

Falconbridge now had effected the grand object; he was next to collect and fettle the miferable refugees : no time was to be loft in accomplifhing this; the month of February was nearly fpent, only three months of dry wea-ther remained for them to clear their land, build their houfes, and prepare their ground for a crop to fupport them the enfuing year ; he therefore difpatched a Greek, who came out in the Lapwing, with fome of the blacks, up to Pa Bofon's, to gather and bring down the people, while we went in the Cutter, taking a few who were at Bance Ifland, to locate an eligible place, for the fettlement.

The fpot they were driven from, was to be preferred to any other part ; but by treaty it was agreed they fhould not fettle there : There were other fituations nearly as good, and better confiderably
than

than the one fixed on; but immediate convenience was a powerful inducement.

Here was a fmall village, with feventeen pretty good huts, which the natives had evacuated from a perfuafion they were infefted by fome evil fpirits; but as they made no objection to our occupying them, we gladly took poffef- fion, confidering it a fortunate circum- ftance to have fuch temporary fhelter for the whole of our people.

When thofe from Pa Bofon's had joined us, Falconbridge called them all together, making forty-fix, including men and women; and after reprefenting the charitable intentions of his coming to Africa, and iffuing to them fuch cloath- ing as were fent out in the Lapwing; he exhorted in the moft pathetic lan- guage, that they might merit by their induftry and good behaviour the notice now taken of them, endeavour to remove the unfavourable prejudices that had gone abroad, and thereby deferve fur- ther favours from their friends in Eng- land; who, befides the cloaths they had already received, had fent them tools of all kinds, for cultivating their land, alfo arms and ammunition to defend them-

felves,

felves, if neceffary; that thefe articles would be brought on fhore when they got a ftorehoufe built; where they would be lodged for their common good and occafional ufe; he then concluded this harangue by faying,—he named the place GRANVILLE TOWN, after their friend and benefactor, GRANVILLE SHARP, Efq. at whofe inftance they were provided with the relief now afforded them.

I never did, and God grant I never may again, witnefs fo much mifery as I was forced to be a fpectator of here: Among the outcafts were feven of our country women, decrepid with difeafe, and fo difguifed with filth and dirt, that I fhould never have fuppofed they were born white; add to this, almoft naked from head to foot; in fhort, their appearance was fuch as I think would extort compaffion from the moft callous heart; but I declare they feemed infenfible to fhame, or the wretchednefs of their fituation themfelves; I begged they would get wafhed, and gave them what cloaths I could conveniently fpare: Falconbridge had a hut appropriated as a hofpital, where they were kept feparate from the other fettlers, and by
his

his attention and care, they recovered in a few weeks.

I always fuppofed thefe people had been tranfported as convicts, but fome converfation I lately had with one of the women, has partly undeceived me: She faid, the women were moftly of that defcription of perfons who walk the ftreets of London, and fupport themfelves by the earnings of proftitution; that men were employed to collect and conduct them to Wapping, where they were intoxicated with liquor, then inveigled on board of fhip, and married to *Black men,* whom they had never feen before; that the morning after fhe was married, fhe really did not remember a fyllable of what had happened over night, and when informed, was obliged to inquire *who was her husband?* After this, to the time of their failing, they were amufed and buoyed up by a prodigality of fair promifes, and great expectations which awaited them in the country they were going to: " Thus," in her own words, " to the difgrace of my mother country, upwards of one hundred unfortunate women, were feduced from England to practice their
iniquities

iniquities more brutifhly in this horrid country."

Good heaven! how the relation of this tale made me fhudder; — I queftioned its veracity, and enquired of the other women who exactly corroborated what I had heard; neverthelefs, I cannot altogether reconcile myfelf to believe it; for it is fcarcely poffible that the Britifh Government, at this advanced and enlightened age, envied and admired as it is by the univerfe, could be capable of exercifing or countenancing fuch a Gothic infringement on human Liberty.

Immediately after we had fixed on this Place for the fettlement, I fingled out one of the beft huts for my own refidence; where I remained nigh a month, though I did not fleep on fhore the whole time : About a fortnight I continued to go on board the Cutter at night, when it was neceffary to fend her to Bance Ifland; I then had a kind of bedftead, not unlike an hofpital cradle, erected in my hovel; but the want of a door was fome inconvenience, and as no deal, or other boards could be procured for the purpofe, I made a coun-

try

try mat fupply the place—for I now find 'tis neceffary to accommodate myfelf to whatever I meet with, there being but few conveniencies or accommodating things in this part of Africa.

The river abounds with fine fifh, and we get abundance of them; which, with rice, wild deer, and fome poultry, forms my common food fince I came to Granville-Town.

In fomething lefs than four weeks we got a large ftore houfe and feveral additional huts for the fettlers built, and had the goods landed from the Lapwing—they confift chiefly of ironmongery, fuch as blackfmiths and plantation tools, a prodigious number of child en's trifling *halfpenny knives*, and fome few dozen fciffars of the fame *defcription*.

I am *charitable enough* to think the *benevolent gentleman*, who purchafed thofe goods, had a double purpofe in view, viz. to ferve his fifter from whom he bought them—and the perfons to whom they are fent; but certainly he was unacquai..ted with the quality of the latter articles, or he muft have known they were very improper gifts of charity.

A. part

A part of the ftore-houfe being partitioned off for us, we took up our abode there whenever it was ready for our reception—it is rather larger, and confequently more cool, which is the only preference I can give it to the laft habitation.

The men all do duty as militia, and we have a conftant guard kept during the night; but the natives feem to dread this fpot fo much, that we fee very few, and I really think we have lefs to fear from them than our own people, who are extremely turbulent, and fo unruly at times, that with difficulty Falconbridge can affuage them, or preferve the leaft decorum.

He was defired by the Company to build a fort, and they fent out fix pieces of cannon, which are now on board. the Lapwing—but omitted to *fend carriages*, and confequently the guns are ufelefs; though if they were compleat, Falconbridge thinks it would not be prudent to truft them with the prefent fettlers, from a belief that they might apply them improperly.

He is alfo requefted by his inftruftions to colleft as many famples of country productions

productions as he can, and he wished to employ some of the people in that way, but none would give their services for less than half a guinea per day which price he has been forced to pay them; this is the greatest instance of ingratitude I ever met with.

We were alarmed a little while since by dreadful shouts, in the vicinity of our town, and supposed the natives meant to attack us; immediately Falconbridge armed his militia, and marched out towards where the noise was heard, they had not gone far when they met three or four *Panyarers*, or man thieves, just in the act of ironing a poor victim they had caught hunting, and the shouts we heard proved to be rejoicings of the banditti.

Falconbridge did not think it advisable to rescue the prisoner by force, or to interfere further than what words would do; and as some of the *Panyarers* spoke English, he remonstrated against the devilish deed they were committing, but to little effect.

They said somebody belonging to the prisoner's town had injured them, and it
was

was the cuftom of their country to re-
taliate on any perfon living in the fame
place with an offender, if they could not
get himfelf, which the prefent cafe was an
example of.

They then carried him away, and in all
probability this man will be deprived of
his liberty while he lives, by the barbarous
cuftoms of his country, for the imaginary
offences of another.

I omitted mentioning in my laft letter,
that the day after we arrived at Bance
Ifland, Mr. William Falconbridge, in confequence of a trifling difpute with his brother, feparated from us, and went into
the fervice of Meffrs. Anderfon's, but his
conftitution was not adapted for this unhof-
pitable climate.

He went down the coaft to York Ifland,
in the river Sherbro, about twenty leagues
diftance, where he was unavoidably expofed to the feverity of the weather, from
which he got a fever and although he
immediately returned to Bance Ifland,
and had every affiftance adminiftered;
yet, I am forry to fay, the irrefiftible
conqueror, *Death*, made all endeavours
fruitlefs, and hurried him to eternity
yefterday,

yefterday, after a fhort illnefs of four days.

The tornados, or thunder fqualls, which fet in at this feafon of the year, preceding the continued rains, have commenced fome time, the vivid intenfe lightning from difmal black clouds, make them awfully beautiful; they are accompanied with violent winds and heavy rains, fucceeded by an abominable ftench from the earth, and difagrecable hiffings and noifes from frogs, crickets, and many other infects which the rains draw out.

Mufquettos alfo are growing fo troublefome, as to oblige us to keep continued fmokes in and about the houfe.

I have not feen any ferpents, but am told there are abundance, and fome very venomous.

Here are a vaft variety of beautiful lizards conftantly about the door catching flies: and I have often feen the changeable camelion.

We have not yet been troubled by any of the ferocious wild beafts which inhabit the mountains of Sierra Leone;
but

but I underftand there are numbers, both tygers and lions, befides divers other kinds.

I have now in fpirits an uncommon infeft, which was caught here a day or two ago, in the aft of ftinging a *Lascar*, (one of the fettlers); it is rather larger than a locuft, covered with a tortoife coloured fhell, has forceps like a lobfter, and thin tranfparent wings like a fly; the bite has thrown the poor Lafcar into a dreadful fever, which I fear will carry him off.

I have three monkies, one a very handfome Capuchin, with a fulphur coloured beard of great length.

Nature feems to have been aftonifhingly fportive in tafte and prodigality here, both of vegetable and animal produftions, for I cannot ftir out without admiring the beauties or deformities of her creation.

Every thing I fee is entirely new to me, and notwithftanding the eye quickly becomes familiarized, and even fatiated with views which we are daily accuftomed to; yet there is fuch a variety here as to afford a continual zeft to the fight.

To

To be frank, if I had a little agreeable fociety, a few comforts, and could
enfure the fame good health I have
hitherto enjoyed, I fhould not be againft
fpending fome years of my life in Africa;
but wanting thofe fweeteners of life, I certainly wifh to return to where they may
be had.

When that will be, is not in my power
at prefent to tell; but if I have a
chance of writing to you again, I then
may be able; in the interim accept an
honeft farewel from

Your affectionate, &c.

LETTER

LETTER IV.

GRANVILLE TOWN, *June* 8, 1791.

" *My dear Madam,*

SINCE my laſt I have been to
the French Factory, viſited ſeveral neighbouring towns, and made myſelf a little
intimate with the hiſtory, manners, cuſ-
toms, &c. of the inhabitants of this part
of Africa, which, it ſeems, was firſt diſcovered by the Portugueſe, who named
it *Sierra de Leone,* or *Mountain of Lions.*

The tract of country now called Sierra
Leone, is a Peninſula one half the year,
and an iſland the other—that is, during
the rains the Iſthmus is overflowed.

The river, which was formerly called
Tagrin, now takes its name from the
country ; at its entrance it is about ten
miles from one Promontory to the other,
but here, it is ſcarcely half that diſtance
acroſs,

acrofs, and a few miles higher up it becomes very narrow indeed.

It is not navigable for large veffels any higher than Bance Ifland, but fmall craft may go a great diftance up.

Befides the iflands I have mentioned, there are feveral others, uninhabited, between this and Bance Ifland.

Granville town is fituated in a pretty deep bay, on the fouth-fide of the river, about nine miles above Cape Sierra Leone,* fifteen below Bance Ifland, and fix from Robana.

Half a mile below us is the town of one *Pa Duffee*; two miles lower down is *King Jemmy's*; and beyond him is *Queen Yamacubba's*, and two or three fmall places; a mile above us *Signior Domingo* lives, and a little higher one *Pa Will.*

I have been at all thefe places, and find a great fimilitude in the appearance of the people, their behaviour, mode of living, building, amufements, &c.

The

* The Cape lies in 8. 28. N. Lat.—12. 30. W. Lon.

The men are tall and ftout, and was it not that their legs are generally fmall in proportion to their bodies, and fomewhat crooked, I fhould call them well limbed.

The mode of treating infants till they are able to walk, accounts for their being bandy legged.

A few days after a woman is delivered, fhe takes her child on her back to where-ever her vocation leads her, with both its legs buckled round her waift, and the calves preffed to her fides, by which means the tender bones are forced from their natural fhape, and get a curve that never after grows out; and thus, the infant is expofed either to the fcorching fun, or any change of weather that hap-pens.

The women are not nigh fo well fhaped as the men, being employed in all hard labour, makes them robuft and clumfy; they are very prolific, and keep their breafts always fufpended, which, after bearing a child or two, ftretches out to an enormous length; difgufting to Euro-peans, though confidered *beautiful* and ornamental here.

They

They are not only obliged to till the ground, and do all laborious work, but are kept at a great diftance by the men, who feldom fuffer a woman to fit down or eat with them.

The day I dined at King Naimbana's, he told me I was the firft woman that ever eat at the fame table with him.

Great refpect and reverence is fhewn to old age, by all ranks of people.

Polygamy likewife is confidered honorable, and creates confequence.

When an African fpeaks of a great man, he or fhe will fay, " Oh! he be fine man, rich too much, he got too much woman."

The higher clafs of people hereabouts, moftly fpeak broken Englifh, which they have acquired from frequent intercourfe with veffels that come to purchafe flaves.

They feem defirous to give education to their children, or in their own way of expreffing it, " Read book, and learn to be *rogue* fo well as white man ;" for they fay, if white men could not read,

or

or wanted education, they would be no better rogues than *black gentlemen.*

I was treated with the utmoft hofpitality at every town I vifited.

Their common food is rice, pepper pot, or palaver fauce, palm nuts, and palm oil ; with the latter both fexes anoint their bodies and limbs daily, though it does not prevent them from fmelling vaftly ftrong.

Wherever I went, there was commonly a fowl boiled or broiled for me : I liked the pepper pot, it is a kind of foup made with a mixture of vegetables highly feafon-ed with falt and red pepper.

Their houfes are much like thofe I have heretofore defcribed, but very low, they are irregularly placed, and built either in a fquare or circular form ; and as this part of the country is thinly inha-bited, each town contains very few houfes.

The inhabitants are chiefly Pagans, though they credit the exiftence of a God, but confider him fo good that he cannot do them an injury ; they therefore

fore pay homage to the *Devil,* from a belief that he is the only Supernatural Being they have to fear; and I am informed they have confecrated places in different parts of the woods, where they make annual facrifices to him.

Cleanlinefs is univerfally obferved; their fimple furniture, confifting generally of a few mats, wooden trenchers and fpoons made by themfelves, are always tidy, and their homely habitations conftantly clean fwept, and free from filth of any kind : nor do I think nature has been fo unkind to endow thofe people with capacities lefs fufceptibie of improvement and cultivation than any other part of the human race.

I am led to form this conjecture, from the quicknefs with which even thofe who cannot underftand Englifh, comprehend my meaning by geftures or figns, and the aptnefs they have imitated many things after me.

Their time is calculated by plantations, moons, and days; the reafon of the firft is, they clear a new field once a year, and if afked the age of a child, or any thing elfe, they will anfwer, fo many plantations,

in

in place of years : they regiſter their moons by notches on a piece of wood which is carefully hanged up in ſome particular part of the houſe.

Their chief amuſement is dancing: in the evening men and women aſſemble in the moſt open part of the town, where they form a circle, which one at a time enters, and ſhews his ſkill and agility, by a number of wild comical motions.

Their muſic is made by clapping of hands, and a harſh ſounding drum or two, made out of hollowed wood covered with the ſkin of a goat.

Sometimes I have ſeen an inſtrument reſembling our guitar, the country name of which is *bangeon.*

The company frequently applaud or upbraid the performer, with burſts of laughter, or ſome odd diſagreeable noiſe; if it is moonſhine, and they have ſpirits to drink, theſe dances probably continue until the moon goes down, or until day light.

The *Timmany* dialect is commonly ſpoke here, though the nation ſo called is ſome diſtance to the northward.

The

The natives account for this in the
following way,

Many years ago the Burces, a tribe of
people formerly living upon the banks of
the river Sierra Leone, were conquered
and drove away to other parts of the
country by the Timmany's, who, having
poffeffed themfelves of the land, invited
many ftrangers to come and live among
them.

The Timmany's being again engaged in
war, which the inhabitants of Sierra Leone
did not chufe to join in, they therefore
alienated the connection, and declared
themfelves a diftinct nation, and have
been confidered as fuch ever fince.

Every chief or head man of a town is
authorized from the King to fettle local
difputes,—but when difagreements of confequence arife between people of feparate
places, then a Palaver is fummoned to the
refidence of the complainant, when the
King attends or not as fuits him ; but if
inconvenient to go in perfon, he fends his
his Palaver-man, who carries the King's
fword, cane, or hat, as a fignal of inau-
guration, to his office.

When

When all the parties are met, they enquire into the butinefs of their meeting, and a majority of voices determine who has *reason* of his or her fide.

If the crime is fornication, the punifhment is flavery, unlefs the offender can ranfom him or herfelf, by paying another flave, or the value in goods.

It is cuftomary when the *Judges* cannot procure fufficient proof, to oblige the party accufed to take a poifonous draught, called Red Water—this potion is prepared by the *Judges* themfelves, who make it ftrong or weak, as they are inclined by circumftances—if ftrong, and the ftomach does not rejeet it inftantaneoufly, de th foon enfues—but if weak, it feldom has any other effeet than a common emetic.

At the laft town I vifited, the head man's favorite woman, had a beautiful *mulatto* child, and feeing me take much notice of it, he faid. " God amity fen me dat peginine, true, fuppofe he no black like me, nutting for dat, my woman drinkee red water, and fuppofe peginine no for me, he dead."

I could

I could not help fmiling at the old fool's credulity, and thinking how happy many of my own countrywomen would be to rid themfelves of a fimilar ftigma, fo eafily.

Crimes of larger magnitude, fuch as *witchcraft,* murder, &c. are punifhed in the fame way, i. e. the criminal is obliged to drink of this liquor, unlefs there be evidence fufficiently ftrong to acquit or condemn him: when that is the cafe, if convicted, he either fuffers death, or is fold as a flave.

On the oppofite fhore lives a populous nation called the Bulloms, whofe King I had occafion to mention in a former letter. I have been at only one of their fettlements, a place directly over againft us, belonging to a man named Dean.

The people appear more inclined to induftry than the Sierra Leonians, which a ftranger may readily difcern, by a fuperior way their houfes are furnifhed in.

I am told it is a fertile country, and the inhabitants make fo much rice, that they are able to fell a quantity annually.

In

In the neighbourhood of Dean's Town, at a place called Tagrin Point, was formerly an Englith factory, belonging to one Marhall; but he unluckily got into a difpute with the natives, who drove him away, and pillaged his goods; they are a barbarous implacable fet of people.

This is all the hiftory I have learnt of the Bulloms, therefore fhall return to my own fide of the water.

We have had heavy tornadoes and falls of rain for feveral we ks, and I yet enjoy my health as well, if not better, than I did for feveral years paft in Europe.

Deaths are not frequent among the natives; indeed I have not heard of one fince we arrived.

Their national difeafes are few; probably anointing themfelves as they do with palm oil, makes them lefs liab e to evil confequences from the unhealthy putrid vapour that almoft conftantly hovers about thefe mountains; the poifonous effects of which carries off numbers of foreigners.

About ten days ago the mafter of the cutter went to Bance Ifland, where he
drank

drank too freely, and returning a little indifpofed, fignified a wifh of going to the French factory for medical affiftance.

Falconbridge having had fome difference with this man, therefore, left he might wrong conftrue any offers to ferve him, without hefitation complied with his defire, and he immediately fet out in the cutter to Gambia, Falconbridge and myfelf accompanying him.

The diftance being but fix miles, and a frefh fea breeze, we foon ran up.

Mr. Rennieu not only received us with the politenefs of a Frenchman, but with kindnefs and friendfhip.

When he faw the mafter of the Lapwing, he faid to me, " Madam, Captain Kennedy (for that was his name) will never leave Africa, but in two or three days time he will come under my *big tree.*"

I did not inftantly comprehend him, which the Frenchman perceived, and explained himfelf by faying, ' under the large tree I faw a little diftance off was the burying ground and' added he, " there is fomething in the countenance
of

of Kennedy denoting his diffolution to be near at hand; and I am perfuaded the man cannot live more than two or three days."

I took care not to mention or hint to Kennedy what Mr. Rennieu faid to me, left the force of imagination might kill him —however, in fpite of all our endeavours, the prophecy was fulfilled; a fevere fever came on the fame night, and the fecond day he was a corpfe.

There was no accommodation for fleep-ing on fhore at the Factory, which Mr. Rennieu could offer us—we were, confe-quently, obliged to fleep on board.

I could not think of allowing the poor fick man to be expofed to the inclemency of night air, and infifted on his taking a birth in the cabin—nor could I think of continuing in the cabin while he was ill, left his diforder might be infectious; and the only alternative was to lay upon deck, or in the hold.

The former being moft preferable, our mattreffes were fpread at night under the awning, where we lay; but I took the pre-caution to wrap myfelf up in a flannel gown,

gown, and cover'd my head with a cap of the fame—was it not for that, in all probability, I muſt have added to the number under Mr. Rennieu's big tree.

For two nights we lay on deck, and each of them, we were unlucky enough to have violent tornadoes; during the ſtorm I threw two large blankets over me, and though the rain penetrated through both, yet my flannel gown and cap intercepted it and prevented me from getting wet, except my feet, which I bathed in ſpirits when the tornado was over, and thus, I believe, eſcaped any bad conſequences; but being under the neceſſity of ſtaying another night at Gambia, I did not chuſe to experience the good effects of my blankets a third time, and accepted an invitation which the Captain of an American had made us—to take a bed on board his ſhip.

Immediately after the corpſe was removed, we had the Lapwing ſcoured, waſhed with vinegar, and ſmoaked with tobacco and brimſtone, to free her from every ſuſpicion of dangerous infection.

I muſt avail myſelf of the preſent moment to give you ſome deſcription of Gambia Iſland.

It

It is fmall and low, not two miles in circumference, fituated in the midft of fwamps and marfhes, from whence a continued ftench comes fufficient to choak a carrion crow—'tis wonderful how many human beings could pitch on fuch a place to live in.

The Europeans there have all complexions as if they were fed on madder and faffron.

Their manner of living is flovenly and hoggifh, though they feem to have plenty of frefh ftock, and provifions of almoft every kind—they are very inactive and indolent, which I am not aftonifhed at, for fuch muft enfue from the laffitude produced by the unhealthinefs of the place.

The buildings are of mean and difrefpectable appearance, being a pile of grafs and fticks clumfily put together.

They have a factory fhip, and few goods are kept on fhore, from a fear of being furprifed and robbed by the natives.

Formerly the Ifland was protected by a company of French foldiers, but the vaft
and

and rapid mortality, deterred their government from fending frefh fupplies.

Rennieu, however, preferves a kind of confequence, and keeps his neighbours in awe by a number of ftrange legerdemain tricks he has learnt, fome of which he fhews whenever he has vifitors.

After feeing Gambia, I confider Granville Town a delightful fpot, where we have none of thofe fwampy low grounds; but a reviving fea breeze that cheers us every day, which is almoft fpent before it reaches them; I fuppofe this muft be owing to the heavy denfe atmofphere that oppofes its progrefs, for diftance cannot be the caufe.

Since the rains commenced, the nights grew alternately cooler, indeed I find a blanket very comfortable; even during the dry weather (when I had room to breathe), I found night many degrees colder than day; but it is now, at times, fo cold, that I am glad to find a fire.

This fudden tranfition from heat to cold, and from cold to heat, I am rather difpofed to think, accounts for the turpitude of the climate, at all events

it

it certainly is one of the moſt conſiderable cauſes.

From a fear my inadequatenefs to give hiſtorical delineations, will expoſe me to your criticifm, I have to beg you will look over any rhapſodies with lenity; *this* is all I can hope for, — *that* all I dread.

Falconbridge thinks of leaving Afiica the middle of this month; the lofs of Kennedy, want of proviſions fit for taking to fea, and the late Mate (now Maſter of the cutter), and ſeveral of our people being ſick, difconcerts us a good deal: but we are told the rains will be conſiderably worſe, and every day will render it more dangerous and difficult to get off the coaſt: Falconbridge is determined to do his beſt, and get away as quick as poſſible.

Oh my friend! what happineſs ſhall I feel on ſeeing Old England again; and if it pleaſes God for us o arrive fafe, the diffi-culties, dangers, and inconveniences I have ſurmounted, and have yet to encounter, will only ſerve me to laugh at.

Your's, &c. &c.

LETTER

LETTER V.

London, *Sept.* 30, 1791.

My dear Friend,

I HAVE many apologies to make for not giving you earlier intelligence of our arrival; but my excuſes are good ones, and no doubt will convince you my ſilence cannot be attributed to the ſlighteſt ſhadow of negligence or forgetfulneſs.

We arrived at Penzance, in Cornwall, the 2d inſtant, when (not being able to walk), I was carried in an arm chair by two men, to the houſe of *Mrs. Dennis*, who friendly invited us to ſhelter under her hoſpitable roof, while we remained there.

The hurry and fatigue of moving, with the reſtraint one cuſtomarily feels, more
or leſs

or lefs of, upon going to a ftrange houfe, prevented me writing you the firft day; but the day fubfequent I wrote as follows:

My dearest Madam,

 " I AM returned to this bleffed land; join with me in fervent prayer and thankf-giving to the Author of all good works, for his miraculous protection and good-nefs during a circuitous paffage of nigh three months, replete with hardfhips un-precedented, I believe in any voyages heretofore related, the particulars of which I muft take fome other opportunity to fur-nifh you with."

Here I made a full paufe; and, after thinking and re-thinking for near half an hour, whether I fhould fubfcribe my name and fend it to the poft, a thought ftruck me,—" Why! I fhall be in London in eight or ten days, when it will be in my power to fend a narration of what has hap-pened fince I laft wrote Mrs. ———; and if I write now, I fhall only excite curiofity, and keep her in unpleafant fufpence for fome time; fo it is beft to poftpone writing till 1 can do it fully."

Now,

Now, in place of eight or ten days, it was almoft three weeks before we reached this metropolis; and fince I arrived, my time has been wholly occupied in receiving inquifitive vifitors, and anfwering a few pertinent, and a number of ridiculous queftions.

I could make many other reafonable pleas, in behalf of my filence, but truft what is already faid will be amply fatisfactory; fhall therefore forbear making any further apologies, and proceed with an account of myfelf fince I laft wrote to you.

The 16th of June we went to Robana to take leave of the *Royal Family*, and to receive the young Prince John Frederic on board; all this we accomplifhed, and failed the fame day.

Naimbana feemed unconcerned at parting with his fon, but the old Queen cried, and appeared much affected.

The Prince was decorated in an old blue cloak, bound with broad gold lace: which, with a black velvet coat, pair of white fatin breeches, a couple of fhirts, and two or three pair of trowfers, from a
compleat

compleat inventory of his ftock of cloaths, when he left Africa.

The old man gave John all the cafh he had, amounting to the *enormous sum* of eight Spanifh dollars (about thirty-five fhillings) ; and juft when we were getting under way, faluted us with twelve guns, from fome rufty pieces of cannon, laying on the beach without carriages.

The Lapwing was badly equip'd for fea ; the crew and paffengers amounted to nine : four of the former were confined with fevers, confequently there were only four, (and but one a failor) to do the fhip's duty.

Mr. Rennieu gave me a goat and half a dozen of fowls : King Naimbana put a couple of goats, and a dozen of fowls on board for his fon.

Befides thefe, I purchafed fome poultry, and when we failed, confidered ourfelves poffeffed of a pretty good ftock, confifting of three goats, four dozen of fowls, a barrel of flour, half a barrel of pork, and a barrel of beef.

We

We had not been at fea a week, when all our live ftock were wafhed or blown overboard, by repeated and impetuous tornadoes—fo that we had not a thing left but the flower and falt provifions; however, we were in hopes of getting in a few days to Saint Jago, one of the Cape De Verd Iflands, where the lofs of our ftock might be replaced.

In this we were difappointed, for inftead of a few days, a continued interruption of calms and boifterous weather, made it fix weeks before we reached that Ifland; during the whole of which time I was confined to my cabin, and moftly to my bed, for it rained inceffantly.

After being about three weeks at fea, our fick got clear of their fevers, but were fo emaciated as to be unfit for any duty, *except eating*, and though there was no food fit for convalefcent perfons on board, yet the coarfe victuals we had ftood no chance with them, and made it neceffary to put all hands to an allowance.

Upon enquiring into the ftate of our provifions, we found they had been la-
vifhly

vifhly dealt with ; there was not more than one week's full allowance of meat, and fcarcely four days of flour remaining.

Thefe were alarming circumftances, for we had two thirds further to go, than we had then come, toward Saint Jago.

I did not felfifhly care for the want of beef or pork, as I had not tafted either fince we failed from Sierra Leone; but I lamented it for others.

All hands were reftricted to a quarter of a pound of beef or pork, and a fmall tea-cup full (rather better than a gill) of flour per day.

What would have been more dreadful we fhould have wanted water, was it not for the rains; the worms having imperceptibly penetrated our water cafks, all the water leaked out, except a fmall cafk, which would not allow us more than a pint each, for three weeks.

My tea-cup of flour, mixed with a little rain water and falt, boiled to a kind of pap, when the weather would
admit

admit a fire, otherwife raw, was, believe me, all my nourifhment for ten
days, except once or twice, when fome
cruel unconfcionable wretch robbed me
of the homely morfel, I was forced to
tafte the beef.

The week before we arrived at St.
Jago, our Carpenter, who had been ill,
and was on the recovery, relapfed, and
died in twenty-four hours ; which circumftance terrified me exceedingly, leaft our
afflictions were to be increafed with fome
peftilential difeafe ; however, no fimilar
misfortunes attended us afterwards.

We arrived at Porta Praya in St Jago,
I think, the 25th of July, when Falconbridge immediately went on fhore to
obtain fufferance to remain there a few
days, while he re-victualled and watered.

An officer met him as he landed, and
conducted him to the chief magiftrate of
the Port, who lives in a Fort on top of a
hill which commands the harbour.

Falconbridge was well received, his
requeft granted, and he and myfelf were
invited to dine at the Fort next day—
but he was informed, provifions were
not

not to be had for any price—a fleet
of European fhips had juft failed from
thence, and drained the country of almoft every kind of eatable.

After being fix weeks confined in the
narrow bounds of the Lapwing s cabin,
and moft of the time in bed, f d as I
was upon fcanty wr tched food, notwith-
ftandin. the benignitv ot heaven had preferved me from difeafe of any kind, you
will not queftion my energy of mind and
body being confiderably enervated; indeed, fo enfeebled did I fee myfelf, that
it was with much difficulty I accompanied
Falconbridge to dinner at the Conful's,
for fo the Chief Officer of Porto Praya
is termed; but the diftance I had to walk
was fhort, and with the help of a Portuguefe officer on one fide, and my hufband
on the other, I accomplifhed it tolerable
well.

The company confifted of the Portuguefe and French Confuls, five Portuguefe and two French gentlemen, two
Portuguefe ladies, Falconbridge, and myfelf.

None of the foreigners fpoke Englifh,
fo you will readily guefs we but poorly
amufed

amufed or entertained each other; through the medium of a linguift who attended, any compliments, queftions or anfwers, &c. &c. were conveyed to and fro.

Our dinner was very good, and I had prudence enough to be temperate, having often heard of fatal confequences from indulgencies in fimilar cafes.

During dinner we had excellent claret and madeira, but no wine was drank after; directly as the cloth was removed, tea was introduced in the moft uncommon way I ever faw or heard of before; it was brought in china mugs, containing three pints each, and every perfon was prefented with one of thofe huge goblets.

I had not tafted tea for feveral weeks, neverthelefs, one third of this quantity was more than I chofe to fwallow—but with aftonifhment I beheld others make a rapid finifh of their allowance.

Having thus inundated their ftomachs, every one arofe, and our hoft defired the linguift to acquaint me they were going to repofe themfelves for a while, and if I was inclined to follow their example, a fofa,

or

or bed was at my fervice ; being bed fick-
ened, I declined the offer, and chofe, in
preference to ftretch my feeble limbs with
gentle walking in a pleafant portico, fronting the fea; for I had gathered ftrength
enough in the few hours I was on fhore,
to walk alone.

The company having indulged about an
hour in their habitual flothfulnefs, re-af-
fembled; we were invited to take a bed
on fhore, but Falconbridge learnt, the
generality of people were thievifhly difpofed, and for that reafon did not chufe
to fleep from the cutter; and you know
it would have been very uncomfortable for
me to remain without him, among a parcel
of ftrangers, when we could not underftand what one or other faid; befides, I had
other prudential objections for not remaining without Falconbridge, which the hor-
ror of our loathfome bark could not conquer.

After this, we remained four days in
Porto Praya Road, during which, I went
on fhore frequently.

The town is fituated on the fame height
with the fort.

They

They have a Romiſh chapel, (for the inhabitants are all Roman Catholics) market
place and jail, built of ſtone, and covered
with ſlate in the European way—the other
buildings are moſtly of wood and thatch,
after the African manner.

The French Conful has his houſe within
the fort, which is a decent good looking
building, as is the Portugueſe Conful's;
but this is of ſtone, and that of wood.

The people of moſt countries have their
peculiar modes of habiting themſelves, but
ſurely the cuſtom of Porto Praya is more
odious than any other ;—in meeting a hundred men, two are not to be ſeen dreſſed
alike—perhaps one will have a coat thrown
over his ſhoulders without occupying the
ſleeves; another a woman's petticoat drawn
round his neck, with his arms through the
pocket holes, and ſo on, except the higher
ranks.

The women dreſs rather more uniform-
ly; they wear very ſhort petticoats, and
tight jackets, of a coarſe linen, like Of-
naburg, but no *ſhifts*; I mean the lower
claſs, or natives, who are moſtly black,
or of mixed complexions; for the few European ladies there, are genteely habited

bited with fine India muflins, and their hair neatly plaited, and put up in filk nets.

A narrow, handfome kind of cotton cloth is manufaQured at St. Jago ; I went to one of the manufaƈtorics, and purchafed feveral pieces; they are in great eftimation, and fell for a high price—I paid five and fix dollars a piece, (about two yards and a half; for thofe I bought.—The loom they are wove in refembles our garter loom.

I underftood the inhabitants raife their own cotton, and have feveral fmall fugar works, which makes a fufficiency of fugar for the confumption of thofe iflands, but no quantity for expoitation.

The Governor refides at a town named St. Jago, a confiderable diftance from Porto Praya, and on the oppofite fide of the ifland, which put it out of our power to vifit it.

The Conful at Porto Praya is his Vicegerent, but has his authority from Portugal ; there appeared to me a great want of government among the people, notwithftandwithftanding a ftrong military force is kept there.

We got a fuperabundance of fine fifh while we remained at St. Jago, which was a fortunate circumftance—for our intelligence refpecting the fcarcity of provifions was perfectly true.

With our utmoft endeavours we could not procure but two goats and two dozen of fowls to take with us to fea; and thofe I was obliged to purchafe with fome of my wearing apparel, which was preferred to money; or, I fhould fay, they were not to be had for money.

Bread and falt provifions were not to be had in the fmalleft quantity, for any price; however, we purchafed a number of cocoa nuts, which they have in plenty, as a fubftitute for bread.

With thefe trifling and ordinary fea-ftores we departed from Porto Praya, the 30th of July, trufting by œconomical management, to make them ferve till we reached fome other port.

I recovered my ftrength and fpirits confiderably during the fhort time we were at
that

that place, as did all our fick; indeed it was neceffary and lucky, for it enabled us to contend againft misfortune, and conquer the hardfhips, and inconveniencies, which afterwards attended us.

We had fine moderate weather the firft twenty-four hours, and got the length of St. Vincent, one of the fame iflands, where, falling calm, we came to anchor.

Some of the people went on fhore, thinking to kill a few birds; and fuppofing the ifland uninhabited, it being a fmall barren place, without a tree or fhrub of any fort, a kind of fern excepted, fo that no houfes could be there, and efcape our notice.

The boat's crew had fcarcely landed, when we were greatly aftonifhed and alarmed to behold from the cutter (for we lay no diftance off the fhore) five *naked human beings*, who had juft ftarted up from behind a hilloc, running towards them—however, our fears were quickly abated, by feeing the boat returning.

The mafter was one that went on fhore, and he underftood a little Portuguefe, in which language thefe victims to barbarity

barity addreſſed, and told him, they had, ſeveral months paſt, been baniſhed from an adjacent iſland, called Mayo, and landed where they then were in the deplorable condition he beheld them.

The Lapwing was the firſt veſſel that had anchored there ſince their exilement, and they begged and prayed we would take them off—they did not care where!

This we could not do with any kind of diſcreetneſs, from the danger of ſtarving them and ourſelves.

They conſiſted of three men and two women, and we muſtered two petticoats and three pair of trowſers for them.

I was curious to know ſomething more of the poor wretches, and went with Falconbridge and the Maſter on ſhore.

Before we landed, they had retired behind the hilloc, and we ſent forward their cloathing, that they might be dreſſed by the time we came up.

We found them in the act of broiling fiſh over a fire made of dry fern, which

was

was the only fuel they could poffibly have.

Our Skipper afked, if they had any houfes? but was anfwered in the negative; and pointing to the heaven and the earth, fignifying *this* was their bed, and *that* their covering; he then enquired, how they fubfifted? and for what they were banifhed?

To the firft they replied,—When put on the Ifland, fifhing lines, hooks, and implements for ftriking fire, were given them, through which means they fupported themfelves; there was plenty of fifh, and a good fpring of water; but faid they, " we have not tafted bread fince we left Mayo."

To the fecond, no further anfwer could be obtained, than their having offended the Governor of Mayo, who was a *Black* man.

They were miferably emaciated, and a haplefs melancholy overhang'd their countenances.—When we firft came up, joyful fmiles beamed through the cloud, which foon darkened when they learnt there was no profpect of being relieved.

They

They followed us to the boat, and I really believe, if they had been armed, would have taken her from us : as it was, our men were obliged to ufe violence, and turn them out, for all hands had jumped in, and attempted to get off.

We offered to take any one of them, but not one would confent to feparate or fhare any good fortune the whole could not partake of.

When we got clear from the fhore, they parfued us up to their necks in water, crying and howling fo hideoufly, that I would have given the wor d! (were it at my difpofal, if it was either in our power to bring them away, or that I had not feen them.

Here we remained all night, and till three o'clock the day following, when a light favourable breeze enabled us to fail; before our departure, we fent the convicts an iron pot, for cooking, and a few fifhing utenfils, which was all we could poffibly fpare them.

To the northward of St. Vincent's, about eight or nine miles, is St. Anthony, **another**

another of the Cape de Verd Iflands, which we had to pafs clofe by.

The wind was very weak, but every one imagined there was enough of it to take us clear off that Ifland before morn-ing ; whether that was not the cafe, or whether things were badly managed, I fhall not decidedly fay, though I have a decided opinion on the fubject; for to-wards four o'clock in the morning, being uncommonly reftlefs, I thought, as the veffel appeared very quiet, and the moon fhone beautifully bright, I would get up and fet upon deck for a while.

Perhaps merciful Providence directed this,—for the like I never did before or fince ; and had I not, in all probability we muft have been driven againft the rude rocks of St. Anthony, and God only knows what would have been the con-fequence, as I was the only perfon awake.

The firft thing I faw, upon lifting my head out of the cabin, was thofe lofty per-pendicular rocks pending almoft directly over us, and not a man upon deck but King Naimbana's fon, and him faft afleep.

" Good

" Good God !" cried I, " Falconbridge, we are on fhore!"

He inftantly fprung up, and called all hands, who got the boat out, and with the utmoft exertion towed us off a fmall diftance.

When day light came on, our danger appeared more forcibly, for, notwithftand-ing the oars had been diligently employed an hour and an half, we were not two hundred yards from the Ifland.

Some faid it was a current; others, it was the land which influenced or attracted us: but what the real reafons were I know not; this only I can tell you,—after try-ing every poffible means to no purpofe, till four o'clock in the afternoon, when the men complaining their ftrength was exhaufted, and they could do no more, it was agreed to abandon the Lapwing, and look out for a place where we might land before night, and thereby fecure fafety for our lives, if the veffel could not be preferved.

Accordingly every one was defired to get into the boat, but we found fhe was too fmall to carry us all at once; and two

of

of the failors confented to ftay till fhe
could make a fecond trip.

Falconbridge and myfelf got in, taking
with us a few fhiftings of cloaths and our
bedding; we then rowed to the land, and
after pulling to and fro for near two
hours, could not difcover a fingle fpot
where there was a poffibility of landing;
during which time, we obferved the Cutter
drifting faft toward the fhore, and expected every moment to fee her ftrike.

Defpondency was vifibly pictured in
every face !—" What fhall we do, or what
is beft to be done ?' was the univerfal
cry.

Confcious of a woman's infignificance
in fuch matters, I was filent till then;
when finding a general vacancy of opinion
among the men, I ventured to fay—" Let
us return to the Lapwing, and put our
truft in him who is all fufficient, and whofe
difpenfations are always unqueftionably
juft."

To this forlorn propofition every one
affented; but faid it was only deferring
the evil moment a few hours, for we
fhould certainly have to truft to our boat

very

very fhortly again, unlefs a breeze came off the land.

After getting on board it was fettled—one perfon fhould watch while the reft refrefhed themfelves with fleep, that they might be fomewhat able to encounter the looked-for fatigues of the night.

For my part, I did not in the leaft incline to fleep, but with watchful eyes and aching heart, awaited the expected moment when eight of us were to commit ourfelves, in a fmall open boat, to the mercy of the ungovernable ocean.

Many reflections preffed upon me, but one more powerful than any—"that our dilemma was probably a mark of divine vengeance, for not relieving the diftreffed people at St. Vincent's."

I often afked the watch, if we neared the rocks; fometimes he anfwered in the affirmative, and fometimes doubtfully—but faid we feemed to drift coaftways withall; and he believed there was a ftrong current fetting to the fouthward.

About twelve o'clock Falconbridge came on deck, when I mentioned this
information

information to him : he then took notice himfelf, and found it really fo.

All hands were immediately turned out, and the boat again manned to tow our bark with the current, for though it had not been obferved, we were doubtlefs working againft it all the preceding day.

This proved a propitious fpeculation; in about four hours we could fee the fouth-weft end of the Ifland, and at the fame time had got near a mile off the land.

What a change of countenance was now on board : I felt my bofom fill with gratitude at hearing the glad tidings !

General tokens of joy and congratulations paffed from one fhip-mate to another; and when daylight appeared, inftead of gloom and forrow, every cheek blufh'd cheerfulnefs.

We then found ourfelves clear of the Ifland, and having a fine moderate breeze, bid adieu to the African coaft ; neverthelefs our troubles did not end here.

After

After running to the Weſtward eight and forty hours, a tremendous ſtorm came on, and continued to increaſe in violence for five days.

This had ſcarcely abated, when it was ſuccceded by another, nearly as bad—which however ran us as far as Fayal, one of the Azores, or Weſtern Iſlands, where we arrived the 18th of Auguſt.

I do not mean to take up your time with a deſcription of thoſe ſtorms, or a detail of our ſufferings, ſince we left St. Anthony, till our arrival at Fayal, though I muſt not paſs over them wholly unnoticed.

Every horror the moſt fertile ideas can picture a ſea ſtorm with, aggravated the former ; and, conſequently augmenting the miſeries of the latter, rendered them almoſt unbearable and paſt repreſentation.

God knows they would have been bad enough without ; for the day we reached Fayal, about two pounds of ſalt beef and half a dozen cocoa nuts, were all the proviſions we had left.

We remained there a week, and were hoſpitably entertained by Mr. Graham,

the

the Englifh Conful, who had the good-
nefs to infift on our taking a bed at his
houfe, directly as our arrival was an-
nounced to him.

Being much bruifed and indifpofed by
our boifterous rough paffage, and eating
food I had not been accuftomed to, prevented me from walking abroad for two
or three days; while thus confined, I was
highly delighted and amufed with admiring
Mr. Graham's beautiful garden adjoining
his houfe, where are almoft all·the fruits
of the torrid, frigid, and temperate zones,
in the greateft perfection ; peaches, apples,
prars, oranges, pine apples, limes, lemons,
citron, grapes, &c. &c. the fineft I ever
faw.

Mrs. Graham treated me with motherly
kindnefs; by her attention, and the
wholefomenefs of the climate, I gained
fo much frefh ftrength and fpirits, that
before I came away, I was able frequently
to walk about the town, and once took
an excurfion into the country, with her
and a party of her friends, to the
feat of a Mr. Perkins, an Englifh gentleman.

We

We all rode on affes, for carriages (if they have any) could not pafs the way we went.

I was pleafed with the reception this gentleman gave us, as well as his polite and generous behaviour.

In our way thither we paffed a number of vineyards ; and, as far as I could judge, the country feemed fruitful.

Befides this excurfion, Mr. and Mrs. Perkins perfuaded me to take one with them, to the Ifland of Pico, about eight miles from Fayal, where they have a valuable vineyard ; and where they affured me, I fhould fee the moft wonderful natural curiofity, in the Azore Iflands; viz. two fprings of water within eighteen feet of each other—one nearly as cold as ice, the other boiling with heat.

When we arrived there, feveral wafher-women were employed in their vocation ; they told me the water was foft, and well adapted for wafhing ; that they made it of what temperature they pleafed, by mixing a proportion of each, and declared they had frequently boiled fifh in the hot well: I had a mind to try the heat by putting

my

my finger in, but found the fteam powerful enough to convince me I fhould be
scalded.

There are public Baths at thofe Wells
well attended by the inhabitants of Fayal;
and the adjacent Iflands; they lay fomewhat to the eaftward, at the foot of the
mountain, which gives its name to this
Ifland.

This is the hi heft mountain I ever faw,
very thickly wooded towards its bafe, but
picturefque, with many gentlemens' feats,
and on the whole vaftly gratifying to the
eye.

It produces a particular and favorite
kind of wood, called *Teixa,* or *Teixo,*
which, from its valuable qualities, no one
is allowed to fell for private ufe, it being
referved by the Queen of Portugal, after
the cuftom of her predeceffors, folely for
the fervice of the Portuguefe government.

I was but a few hours at Pico, and this
was all the information I collected.

There are two nunneries, and a magni-
ficent Romifh church at Fayal, which I vifited.

The

The former were crowded with nuns, and many of them beautiful women.

I saw two who spoke English, with whom I converf'd for some time, and purchafed fev ral artificial flowers, and a few fweat-meats from them.

One of them had all the traces of beauty yet unblemifhed but to a certainty fomewhat tinged by ruinous time; for by her own account fhe muft be far advanced in years.

Upon afking her opinion of a monaftic life, fhe faid, "Madam, I have been within the walls of this convent forty three years, and had I to travel over my life anew, I would prefer the fame path to all others."

But a charming buxom young girl thought otherwife.—She faid, "Can you fuppofe an animated creature, like me, full of youthful fire, was defigned by nature to fpend her days within thefe difmal walls? No! nor can I figure to myfelf, that any one (in fpite of what many may tell you) can find pleafure in burying her-felf alive, and thwarting the purpofes of

her

her creation, for fuch is certainly the cafe with all nuns," and continued fhe : " My parents placed me here at a time when I was not capable of judging for myfelf; nor do I fcruple to fay that my ideas and fancies are fluttering among the amufements and gaieties of the world, and had I my will, my perfon would be there alfo."

I attended the church at mafs time; after fervice was ended, I obferved feveral men bringing in a large fail of a fhip, which had a curious appearance to a ftranger, as I was; but a gentleman prefent faid, " Thofe people have been in the fame ftorm with yourfelves, and they are giving that fail to the church as a thanks offering for their deliverance;" he then fhewed me part of the boat which Captain Inglefield had been faved in, and which was kept here as a record of divine favour to that gentleman.

This circumftance refrefhed my memory with the notorious fufferings and wonder-ful efcape of Captain Inglefield and his boat's crew; and after mentally weighing our misfortunes with his, I fumm'd them both up as follows.

Captain

" Captain Inglefield experienced all the miferies of hunger, fatigue, and oppreffion of fpirits, which fixteen days in an open boat, expofed to the furious untameable wind and fea, without provifion, in momentary expeƐation of being hurried to eternity, could infliƐ, befides the additional horrors produced by ruminating on the haplefs condition of fuch numbers of his fellow creatures, in the fame fituation with himfelf."

" We have been fifty-eight days in a deck'd boat, not twice the fize of Captain Inglefield's—continued rains almoft all the while—three weeks a quarter of a pound of beef, and about half the quantity of flour our allowance—eighteen days more baffled by calms and contrary winds, or beat about by mercilefs ftorms, fed upon mean difagreeable food, and fcarcely enough of that to keep foul and body together; and, what was worfe than all, the apprehenfion of being left morfelefs of any kind of nourifhment; which certainly muft have been the cafe, had we not arrived at Fayal when we did "

Having done this, I compared them with one-another—and though it is unfair to give my decifion, we being too often

apt

apt to magnify our own misfortunes, and always fuppoling them greater than thofe of others; yet I fhall hazard making you acquainted with the conclufion I drew, which, however, was very laconic.

I faid to myfelf, " Captain Inglefield's fufferings are matchlefs, and were it not for the duration, and repetition of mine, they could have but little femblance to one-another."

The fmall pox was committing prodigious ravages among all ranks of people, when we left Fayal; and, I fuppofe, continues ftill fo to do.

A child of the French Conful's lay dangeroufly ill with that difeafe, and he requefted Faconbridge would vifit it; he did fo, and found the infant confined in a fmall clofe room, where every means were taken to fhut out the leaft breath of air.

Falconbridge directly recommended the child to be trought into a large open hall, which was done againft t e abfurd re· monftrances of the Portuguefe Phyfician, who pronounced immediate death to it; however, before our departure we had the
pleafure

pleafure of feeing this innocent babe (who would in all probability, have otherwife fallen a victim to thofe ridiculous notions of treating the fmall pox) quite out of danger; and I truft the precedent will be generally attended to, and may prove equally efficacious.

Many of our countrymen refide there, who are Roman Catholics, and married to Portuguefe ladies, with few exceptions.

I faw two or three Englifh women—perhaps all on the ifland; they feem to have preferved their native manners and cuftoms in high perfection, which the Portuguefe ladies emuloufly try to copy, more efpecially in the article of drefs, than any thing elfe; but in this they are much hinder'd by the jealoufy and narrow ideas of their hufbands, who never fuffer their wives to go abroad, or appear in company with other men, whether fingle or married, without a deep black or white fattin veil that hides not only the face but the body.

In a converfation with one of thefe ladies fhe faid to me " the women of your country muft furely be very happy: they have fo much more liberty than we have, or I believe, than the women of any other country,

country, I wish I was an En lish woman!" I thanked her in behalf of my country women, for her good opinion, but affured her they had their share of thorns and
thistles, as well as those of other countries.

How deeply do I regret our short stay
at Saint Jago and Fayal, difables me from
giving you a more hi"orical and intelligent account of those islands; but I was
long enough at each place to form this
fummary opinion: The latter is, without
exception the most defirable spot I ever
faw ; and the former, as far oppofite as it is
poffible for you to conceive.

Having repaired fuch damage as our veffel had received coming fr m St. Anthony,
and fupplied ourfelves with abundance of
ftores to bring us to this country, we fet
fail from Fayal the 25th of laft month, and
arrived at the time and place before mentioned.

Our paffage was short and unattended
with fuch boifterous weather as we had experienced, yet it was fo ftormy that I was
obliged to keep my bed the whole time :
which circumftance and a cold I caught,
threw me into an indifpofition that I have
not yet recovered from.

The

The day after landing at Penzance, Falconbridge wrote to Mr. Granville Sharp, and by return of Post received his answer, a copy of which I herewith inclose.

" *Dear Sir,*

" T H E agreeable account of the safe arrival of the Lapwing at Penzance, which I received this morning, gives me very particular satisfaction.

" I have communicated your letter to Henry Thornton, Esq. Chairman of the Court of Directors of the *Sierra Leone Company* (for under this title the late St. George's Bay Company is now established, by an act of the last Session of Parliament) and to some of the Directors, and they desire you to come by land as expeditiously as you can, bringing with you in a postchaise, Mrs. Falconbridge and the Black Prince, and also any such specimens of the country as will not be liable to injury by land carriage.

" I inclose (from the Directors) a note from Mr. Thornton's house, for thirty pounds, for which you may easily procure
cash

cafh for your journey, and if more fhould be wanting for ufe of the people of the Lapwing, I have no doubt but Mrs. Dennis (to whofe care I fend this Letter) will have the goodnefs to advance it, as fhe will be reimburfed by return of the Poft, when I receive advice of your draft.

" The Lapwing may be left to the care of any proper perfon whom you may think capable of taking due care of her, until the Directors give farther orders refpecting her.

" I remain with great efteem,

" *Dear Sir,*

" Your affectionate Friend,

" And humble Servant,

" GRANVILLE SHARP."

Mr. Alexander Falconbridge.

In the interim Falconbridge went to Falmouth to procure money for our journey to London.

There he met the Rev. Thomas Clarkfon, that unwearied ftickler for human liberty, with whom, (or at whofe inftimulation)

lation (the abolition of the Slave Trade originated, and at whofe inftance Falconbridge quitted his comfortable fituation at Ludway, to enlift in the prefent (though I fear chimerical) caufe of freedom and humanity.

Mr. Clarkfon is alfo a Director of the Sierra Leone Company, under which title, you find by Mr. Sharp's letter, the late St. George's Bay Company is now called.

He informed Falconbridge that his brother, Lieutenant Clarkfon of the navy, was gone to Nova Scotia, authorifed by government to collect feveral hundred free Blacks and take them to Sierra Leone, where they are (under the care and patronage of the Directors of our new Company) to form a Colony.

It was furely a premature, hair-brained, and ill digefted fcheme, to think of fending such a number of people all at once, to a rude, barbarous and unhealthy country, before they were certain of poffeffing an acre of land ; and I very much fear will terminate in difappointment, if not difgrace to the authors ; though at the fame time, I am perfuaded the motives fprung from minds unfullied with evil meaning.

W.e

We fet out from Penzance the 12th, taking with us the Black Prince, and the following day arrived at Plymouth, where by appointment we met Mr. Clarkfon; after flaying there four days, we went on towards London, flopped at Exeter three days, and arrived here on the 24th.

As foon as our arrival was known, Mr. Thornton (the Chairman , Mr. Sharp, and feveral others of the Directors came to fee us, and after many compliments expreffive with condolence for our misfortunes, and congratulations for our deliverance and fafe arrival, a number of enquiries, &c. &c. Mr. Thornton requefted Falconbridge and the Prince would dine with him, at the fame time gave the latter to underftand he was to confider his (Mr. Thornton's) houfe as his home.

I could not help fecretly fmiling to fee the fervile courtefy which thofe gentlemen paid this young man, merely from his being the fon of a nominal King.

It has flip'd my notice till now to defcribe him to you :—His perfon is rather below the ordinary, inclining to groffnefs, his fkin nearly jet black, eyes keenly intelligent,

ligent, nofe flat, teeth unconnected, and
filed fharp after the cuftom of his country,
his legs a little bandied, and his deport-
ment eafy, manly, and confident withal.
In his difpofition he is furly, but has cunning enough to fmother it where he thinks
his intereft is concerned; he is pettifh and
implacable, but I think grateful and attached to thofe he confiders his friends;
nature has been bountiful in giving him
found intellects, very capable of improvement, and he alfo poffeffes a great thirft
for knowledge.

While with me, although it was feldom
in my power, now and then I amufed
myfelf with teaching him the alphabet,
which he quickly learned, and before we
parted, could read any common print fur-
prifingly well.

He is not wanting in difcernment, and
has already difcovered the weak fide of
his patrons, which he ftrives to turn to
good account, and I dare fay, by his natural fubtilty, will in time advantage himfelf confiderably by it.

They

* This young man returned to Sierra Leone in
July 1793, and died the day after his arrival.

The Directors feem much pleafed with Falconbridge's exertions, have appointed him Commercial Agent to the Company, and he is fhortly to return to Sierra Leone. They are very puffing for me to accompany him, but my late misfortune are yet too frefh in remembrance to content haftily. Indeed, you may fuppofe, I cannot but painfully remember them while the bruifes and chafes produced by the voyage on different parts of my body, continue unhealed. However, it is probable, whether with or againft my will, I muft tacitly affent to hazard a repetition of what I have already undergone.

When matters are wholly fixed you will hear from me, and perhaps I may fhortly have the happinefs of affuring you in perfon how I am,

Your's, &c.

LETTER

LETTER VI.

LONDON, *Nov.* 27, 1791.

My dear Madam,

THE Directors have acted fo honorable and handfome it was not poffible for me to hold out in refufing to return to Sierra Leone, befides increafing Falconbridge's falary near three times what it was, they have voted us a fum of money as an equivalent for the extraordinary fervices they confider he has rendered them, and as a compenfation for our private loffes of cloaths, &c.

But furely mortal never was more harraffed than I have been by their importunities.

They ufed every flattering and enticing argument, the ingenious brain of man is capable of, to no purpofe ;—however, though all their rhetoric could not perfuade me to revifit Africa, their *noble, generous* actions have effected it.

Mr.

Mr. Thornton is a good creature, one of the worthiest men I ever met, he has a ured me, should any accident happen Falconbridge, I shall be well provided for by the Company; he has also, as well as many others of the Directors. made me a profusion of friendly promises and professions. so extravagant that if they came from any other set of men I should look upon them, either as chicanery, or without meaning.

The Court has granted 50l. to be laid out in presents for King Naimbana and his old Queen, and have particularly defired, I shall purchase those for the latter, and present them as from myself, by way of enhancing my consequence.

They have likewise granted another sum for me to lay out in such private stores as I may chuse to take with me for our use after we get to Africa; besides ordering a very handsome supply for the voyage.

A few days ago, I only hinted an inclination to visit my friends at Bristol, before we left England, and Mr. Thornton said I should have a Chaise when I liked, and the expence should be defrayed by the Company. Do you not think these are pretty marks of attention?

We

We have thoughts of fetting out for Briftol in the courfe of next week where I figure to myfelf much of that undefcriptionable pleafure, which lively affectionate minds involantarily feel upon meeting the bofom friends and fportive companions of their youthful days, grown to maturity with hearts and countenances neither altered by abfence, or rufted by corroding time.

But I lament to fay this happinefs will be of fhort duration, being obliged quickly to proceed to Falmouth, where we are to embark on board the Company's fhip Amy, for Sierra Leone.

Adieu.

LETTER

LETTER VII.

FREE TOWN, SIERRA LEONE,

10th April, 1792.

" *My dear Madam,*

HERE I am, once more exposed to the influence of a Torrid Sun, near three thousand miles apart from my dearest friends, experiencing, not only, the inevitable hardships of Colonization, but wallowing in a multiplicity of trouble and confusion, very unnecessarily attached to the infant Colony.

We sailed from Falmouth the 19th of December, and arrived at this place the 16th of February, when we found the Harpy, Wilson, a Company ship, that left England some time after us; but our voyage was prolonged, in consequence of being obliged to stop at Teneriff for a few pipes of Wine.

Immedi-

Immediately on entering the river we were vifited by Captain Wilfon, and after the cuftomary civilities, he told us, feveral Colonial Officers, a few foldiers, and fome independant Settlers came paffengers with him, who were greatly rejoiced at feeing the Amy ; for being all ftrangers, they were at a lofs what to do, and wholly relied on Falconbridge to make good their landing.

In the courfe of converfation many fentences efcaped Captain Wilfon, importing a very unfavourable account of his paffengers, but imagining they proceeded from fome mifunderftanding between them and him, neither Falconbridge or myfelf allowed what he faid, to bias or prejudice us in any fhape.

Captain Wilfon having directed the moft eligible fpot for us to bring up, waited until our anchor was gone, and then returned to his fhip : Falconbridge accompanied him to make his obeifance to the Ladies and Gentlemen on board.

In a fhort time, he was confirmed, our furmife, with regard to difagreements fubfifting between the parties, was well grounded, for they were conftantly fnarl-
ing

ing at each other; but it required very little penetration to arrive at the true fource
of their animofities, and before I proceed
further I muft acquaint you, the Directors have appointed eight perfons to reprefent them, and conduct the management of
their Colony, under the *dignified appellation
of Superintendant and Council.*

It is a pity when making thofe appointments, they had not probed for characters
of worth and refpectability, as fuccefs in
any enterprife greatly hinges on fkilful,
prudent conduct; qualities more efpecially
requifite in an undertaking like this, labor-
ing under a load of enemies, who will, no
doubt, take advantage to blow the fmalleft
fpark of mal-conduct into a flame of error.

Perhaps the Directors imagine they were
particularly circumfpect in their choice of
reprefentatives, if fo, they are grofsly deceived, for never were characters worfe
adapted to manage any purpofe of magnitude than fome whom they have nominated.

Are men of little worth and much infignificance fit to be guardians and ftewards
of the immenfe property required, for
erecting the fabric of a new Colony ? Are
Men,

Men, whofe heads are too fhallow to fupport a little viciffitude and unexpeƈted
imaginary aggrandizement, whofe weak
minds delude them with wrong notions of
their nominal rank, and whofe whole time
is occupied with contemplating their fancied confequence, in place of attending to
the real and interefting defigns of their
miffion, calculated for the executors of
a theory, which can only be put in practice by wife and judicious methods ?

Certainly not ; yet of this defcription are
the greater part who guide and direƈt our
Colony ; a majority of whom came paffengers in the Harpy, and who, intoxicated with falfe ideas of their authority, wifhed to affume the prerogative of controling
Captain Wilfon in managing and govern-
ing his fhip ; but the latter treated their
arrogance with contempt, and confequently grew the diffentions alluded to, which
have fince been the caufe of many difagreeable unpleafant occurrences.

Falconbridge foon returned with Captain and Mrs. Wilfon, whom we had invited to dine with us ; four Honorable
Members of the Council, dreffed *cap a
pie,* in a uniform given them by the Directors

rectors to diftinguifh their rank, came with them, to make their bows to your humble fervant, as the wife of their *superior*, Falconbridge being the eldeft member of this *supreme* body.

A meffage was then fent to King Jemmy (oppofite to whofe town the Amy lay) to announce our arrival to him and King Naimbana (who was there at the time,) requefting they would come on board.

Naimbana, accompanied by Mr. Elliotte and a number of attendants, foon complied with our requeft, but Jemmy (would not be prevailed upon.

The old King was overjoyed at feeing me ; being feated, Falconbridge fhewed him the portrait of his fon,* a prefent from the Directors.

The picture is an admirable likenefs, and the poor Father burft into tears when he faw it.

He ftayed with us five days ; and, notwithftanding every courteous art was ufed to perfuade King Jemmy to
honor

---

* The firft of his family transferd on canvas.

honor us with a vifit, we could not effect it : He once confented on condition I remained in his town a hoftage till he re turned ; this I agreed to, and went on fhore for the intention ; but his people diffuaded him juft as he was going off.

You may remember I mentioned in a former letter, the ground where the *first Settlers* were driven from by King Jemmy, being the moft defirable fituation here- abouts for a fetilement, but by the Palaver it was objected to ; however, with coax- ing, and the irrefiftibility of prefents, King Naimbana was prevailed upon to remove whatever objections there were, and on the 28th of February put us in quiet poffeffion of the very fpot ; which is named *Free Town*, from the *principles* that gave rife to the eftablifhment.*

The fecond day after our arrival, there was a grand Council held on board the
M 3   Amy,

---

* It is fituated on a rifing ground, fronting the fea ; fix miles above Cape Sierra Leone, and eigh- teen from Bance Ifland ; feparated from King Jemmy's town by a rivulet and thick wood, near half a mile through : before the town, is pretty good anchorage for fhipping, but the landing places are generally bad. in confequence of the fhore being bound with iron rocks, and an ugly furge, moft commonly breaking on them.

Amy when their Secretary delivered
Mr. Falconbridge new inftructions from
the Directors, directly counter to thofe
he received in London ; fubjecting him,
in his commercial capacity, to the control of the Superintendant and Council,
and acquainting him, Lieutenant Clarkfon was appointed Superintendant.

This has difconcerted Falconbridge
vaftly, and inclines him to conftrue
their conduct to us in England, as jug-
gle and chichane, for the mere purpofe
of enticing him here, knowing he was
the fitteft, nay only perfon, to fecure
a footing for the Nova Scotia Emigrants;
but I cannot think fo harfhly.

After been here a fortnight, Mr. Clarkfon arrived, with the Blacks from America,
a part of whom came fome days before
him.

When he left Nova Scotia, they amounted to between eleven and twelve hundred,
but during the voyage a malignant fever
infefted the Ships, and carried off great
numbers.

Mr. Clarkfon caught the fever, and
miraculoufly efcaped death, which
would

would have been an irreparable lofs to the Colony, being the only man calculated to govern the people who came with him, for by his winning manners, and mild, benign treatment, he has fo gained her affections and attachment, that he can, by lifting up his finger (as he exprefles it) do what he pleafes with them.

They are in general, a religious temperate, good fet of people; at prefent they are employed in building huts for their temporary refidence, till the lands promifed them can be furveyed; when that will be God only knows; the furveyor being a *Ccunfellor* and *Captain* of our *veteran host*, is of too much confequence to attend to the fervile duty of furveying, notwithftanding he is paid for it.

Few of the Settlers have yet got huts erected, they are moftly encamped under tents made with fails from the different fhips, and are very badly off for frefh provifions; indeed fuch is the cafe with us all, and what's worfe, we have but half allowance of very indifferent falt provifion, and bad worm eaten bread.*

Painfully

* The James, of Briftol, being unfit to proceed her voyage, was condemned and fold at Bance Ifland

Painfully do I fay, nothing promifes
well.—Mr Clarkfon, as Superintendant,
is fo tied up, that he cannot do any thing
without the approbation of his Council,
and thofe opinionated upftarts thwart him
in all his attempts.

He is an amiable man, void of pomp or
oftentation, which his fenatorial affociates
difapprove of exceedingly, from the ridiculous idea that their *dignity* is leffened by
his franknefs.

How truly contemptible it is to fee men
ftickle in this way after foolifh unbecoming confequence blind to the intereft of
their employers, whereby, they muft, without queftion, rife or fall.

Their abfurd behaviour † make them
the laughing ftocks of the neighbouring
Factories, and fuch mafters of flave fhips
as have witneffed their conduct, who muft
certainly

Ifland about this time ; from her a quantity of
beans and other provifions were purchafed which
was a fortunate circumftance for the Colony, then
in a ftarving ftate.

† Few days efcaped without a quarrel, which
fometimes came the length of blows : Members of
Council were daily ordering goods from the fhips,
not wanted, and inevitably to be deftroyed, merely
for the purpofe of fhewing their authority.

certainly be highly gratified with the anarchy and chagrin that prevails through the
Colony.

The Blacks are diſpleaſed that they have
not their promiſed lands; and ſo little do
they reliſh the obnoxious arrogance of their
rulers, that I really believe, was it not for
the influence of Mr. Clarkſon, they would
be apt to drive ſome of them into the
ſea.

The independant European Settlers are
vaſtly diſappointed, and heartily wiſh themſelves back in their own country.

This is not to be wondered at, when in
addition to the calamity of being in a new
Colony, over-run with confuſion, jealouſy,
and diſcordant ſentiments, they are expoſed
to the oppreſſion of wanting almoſt every
neceſſary of life, having no ſhops where
they might purchaſe, or any other medium
of procuring them.

I have only one piece of pleaſing intelligence to give you :—The Colony juſt
now is tolerable healthy; very few deaths
have occurred among the Blacks ſince their
arrival, and but two among the Whites; the
latter

latter were Doctor B———, (our phyſician,)
and the Harpy's gunner.

The gunner's death was occaſioned by
that of the former, who brought on his diſ-
ſolution by inebriety and imprudence;
being a member of the Magiſterial body,
he was buried with all the pomp and ceremony circumſtances would admit of.

While the corpſe moved on in ſolemn
pace, attended by Members of Council, and others in proceſſion, minute guns
were fired from the Harpy; in executing
this, the gunner loſt his arm, of which he
died very ſhortly.

I yet live on ſhip board, for though the
Directors had the goodneſs to ſend out a
canvas houſe purpoſely for me, I have not
the ſatisfaction of occupying it, our *men of
might* having thought proper to appropriate it another way.

Mr. Gilbert, our clergyman, returns
to England in the veſſel I write by, a faſt
ſailing ſchooner, Mr. Clarkſon has pur-
chaſed for the painful, but indiſpenſible
intention of ſending the Directors information of our diſtracted, deplorable ſituation

ation; at the fame time exhorting them
in their *wisdom* to make fome immediate,
efficacious change in our government,
without which their Colony will, irrecover-
ably be ftifled in its infancy.

Mr. Gilbert is a man of mild agreeable
manners, truly religious, without the hypocritical fhew of it; he is univerfally
liked in the Colony, and I am fure his
abfence will be greatly regreted; but
Mr. Clarkfon's indifpofition, rendering
him unable to write fo fully as he wifhes,
or neceffity demands, has prevailed on
him (Mr. Gilbert) to return to England,
and reprefent to the Directors, by word of
mouth, whatever he may neglect to do in
writing.

A party of us will accompany him to
the Banana Iflands, about ten leagues from
hence, where he is in hopes of procuring
frefh ftock, and other neceffary fea ftores,
which are not to be had here for love or
money.

I do not think it will be in my power
to write you from the Banana's; fhall, therefore, clofe this letter with fincere hopes my
next may give you a more favourable account of things.

Farewel, &c. &c.

LETTER

LETTER VIII.

FREE TOWN, *July* 1, 1792.

My dear Friend,

WE accompanied Mr. Gilbert to the Ifland Banana's, where he fucceeded in getting fome frefh ftock, and after ftaying there two days, departed for your quarter of the globe, and I hope is fafe arrived in London long ere now.

The Banana's derives its name from the fruit fo called, which grows there fpontaneoufly, and in great abundance, as do moft tropical fruits.

It is a fmall Ifland, but a wonderfully productive healthful fpot, throngly inhabited by clean, tidy, fociable, and obliging people.

They have a town much larger and more regularly built than any other native town I have yet feen; the inhabitants are moftly vaffals to one Mr. Cleavland,
a Black

a Black man, who claims the fovereignty of the Ifland from hereditary right.

The houfes are chiefly conftructed in a circular form, but of the fame kind of ftuff with thofe I formerly noticed.

In the center of the town is a Palaver, or Court Houfe; here we obferved a bed neatly made up, a wafh hand bafon, clean napkin, and every apparatus of a bed chamber.

This had a very curious appearance; but we were told, the late Mr. Cleveland ufed to indulge himfelf with the luxury of fleeping in this airy place, and the inhabitants fuperftitioufly thinking (though he has been dead more than a year,) he yet invifibly continues the practice, they would not, upon any account, forego the daily ceremony of making up his bed, placing frefh water, &c. as was the cuftom in his life time.

The idolatry fhewn the memory of this man, I make no doubt is greatly encouraged by his fon, as it fecures confequence and popularity to him.

He

He was from home, I therefore did not
fee him, but underftand he is clever, and
(being educated in England) rather polifh-
ed in his manners.

We failed from the Banana's in company with Mr Gilbert, confequently my
time was fo fhort, that I am not able to
give you but a very fuperficial account of
that ifland; but fhall refer you to Lieutenant Mathews's Voyage to Sierra Leone,
where you will find it amply defcribed.
While there, we dined on board an American fhip, commanded by an Irifhman,
who has fince then been here entertaining
himfelf at the expence of our *Senators*.

He invited them all to dine with him,
which being accepted (by every one but
Mr. Clarkfon and Falconbridge,) they were
treated with true Hibernian hofpitality, and
made beaftly drunk.

Our illegitimate fon of Mars was of the
number, who the mafter of the fhip cull'd
out for his butt; he not only played upon
him during dinrer, but afterwards finding
him lull'd into the arms of Morpheus, in
confequence of too much wine, had the
fhip's cook, a flave, dreffed in the noble
Captain's dafhing coat, hat, fword, &c. and
ftationed

ftationed immediately before him with a *mop-stick* on his fhoulder, when the mafter, him-felf, fired two piftols, very heavily charged, within an inch of his ear, and having thus roufed him from his lethargy, the fable cook was defired to fhew with what expert-nefs he could perform the Manual Exercife, which he went through, our *Hero* giving the word of command, to the ridicule of himfelf, and great amufement of his col-leagues and the fhip's crew.

Since this, I have taught a large over-grown female Monkey of mine to go thro' feveral manœuvres of the fame, and have made her exhibit when the Captain came to fee me, who not feeing the diverfion I was making of him, would fometimes take the pains of inftructing her himfelf; but, poor fellow! he has been fadly galled lately, by the arrival of a gentleman from Eng-land, who fuperfedes him in his military capacity.

When I laft wrote to you, I was in hopes my next would atone by a more favoura-ble and pleafing account, for the haplefs defcription I then gave of our new Colony, but alafs! alafs! in place of growing bet-ter, we feem daily advancing towards de-ftruction, which certainly awaits us at no

great

great diſtance, unleſs ſome ſpeedy change
takes place.

There is about twelve hundred ſouls,
including all ranks of people, in the Co
lony, ſeven hundred, or upwards, of whom,
are at this moment ſuffering under the af-
fliction of burning fevers, I ſuppoſe two
hundred ſcarce able to crawl about, and
am certain not more, if ſo many, able to
nurſe the ſick or attend to domeſtic and
Colonial concerns; five, ſix, and ſeven
are dying daily,* and buried with as little
ceremony as ſo many dogs or cats.

It is quite cuſtomary of a morning to
aſk " how many died laſt night ?" Death
is viewed with the ſame indifference as if
people were only taking a ſhort journey, to
return in a few days ; thoſe who are well,
hourly expect to be laid up, and the ſick
look momentarily for the ſurly Tyrant to
finiſh their afflictions, nay ſeem not to care
for life !

After reading this, methinks I hear you
invectively exclaim againſt the country,

and

* About three-fourths of all the Europeans who
went out in 1792, died in the courſe of the firſt
nine or ten months.

and charging those ravages to its unhealthi-
ness; but suspend your judgment for a
moment, and give me time to paint the
true state of things, when I am of opinion
you will think otherwise, or at least allow
the climate has not a fair tryal.

This is the depth of the rainy season,
our inhabitants were not covered in before
it commenced, and the huts they have
been able to make, are neither wind or
water tight; few of them have bedsteads,
but are obliged to lie on the wet ground;
without medical assistance, wanting almost
every comfort of life, and exposed to nau-
ceous putrid stenches, produced by stinking
provision, scattered about the town.

Would you, under such circumstances,
expect to keep your health, or even live
a month in the healthiest part of the world?
I fancy not; then pray do not attribute
our mortality altogether, to baseness of
climate.

I cannot imagine what kind of stuff I
am made of, for though daily in the midst
of so much sickness and so many deaths,
I feel myself much better than when in
England.

I am

I am furprifed our boafted Philan-
thropifts, the Directors of the Company fhould have fubjected themfelves to
the cenfure they muft meet, for fport-
ing with the lives of fuch numbers of ther
fellow creatures, I mean by fending fo
many here at once, before houfes, materials for building, or other conveniences
were prepaied to receive them, and for
not hurrying a fupply after they had been
guilty of this overfight.

But I really believe their error has proceeded from want of information, and liftening with too much credulity, to a pack
of defigning, puritanical parafites, whom
they employ to tranfact bufinefs; I cannot
help thinking fo, nay, am convinced of it,
from the cargoes they have fent out, compofed of goods, no better adapted for an
infant Colony than a cargo of flaves would
be for the London market.

Two veffels arrived from England laft
month, viz the Sierra Leone Packet belonging to the Company; and the Trufty
of Briftol, a large fhip they chartered from
that port; feveral paffengers came in each
of them, in the former were a Member of
Council, a worthy difcreet man; a Botanift, who, I cannot fay any thing of, having

ing feen but little of him; a fugar planter, who is fince gone to the Weft Indies in difguft, and the Gentleman who has fuperfeded our *gallant* Captain, and who, I underftand is alfo a cotton planter, but it is not likely he will have much to do in either of thofe departments for fome time ; his fellow foldiers being moftly dead, and agriculture not thought on.

In the latter came the Store-keeper, with his wife, mother-in law, and a large family of children ; a mineralift, and feveral clerks and tradefmen, in all twenty-three.*

Thofe veffels brought fo little provifions, (with which they fhould have been wholly loaded) that we have not a fufficiency in the Colony to ferve us three weeks. The goods brought out in the Trufty and quantities by other fhips, amounting to feveral thoufand pounds value, at this moment line the fhore, expofed to the deftructive weather and *mercy* of our neighbours, who cannot,

---

* Six returned to England, one left the Colony, and went into the employ of Bance Ifland, and the remainder died in the courfe of three or four months.

not, I am fure, withftand fuch temptation. Thofe remaining on fhip board, I have heard Falconbridge fay, are perifhing by heat of the hold, and damage received at fea. Notwithftanding the Company's property is thus fuffering, and our people dying from abfolute want of nourifhment, Mr. Falconbridge has been refufed the Sierra Leona Packet to go in queft of cattle, and otherwife profecute the duties of his office as Commercial Agent. She is the only veffel fit for the bufinefs ; but it is thought neceffary to fend her to England ; yet, if things were ordered judicioufly, fhe might have made one ferviceable trip in the mean while, and anfwered three defirable purpofes by it : relieve the Colony, bartered away goods that are fpoiling, and pleafe the Directors by an early remittance of African productions; in place of this fhe has only been ufed as a *Pleasure Boat,* to give a week's airing at fea, to *Gentlemen* in perfect health.

Mr. Falconbridge has had no other opportunity but this to do any thing in the commercial way; the Directors no doubt, will be difpleafed, but they fhould not blame him ; he is placed altogether under the control of the Superintendant and Council,

Council, who throw cold water on every propofal of the kind he makes. His time is at prefent employed in attending the fick, particularly thofe of fcrophulous habits, while our military gentleman, who has acquired by experience fome medical knowledge, attends thofe afflicted with fevers, &c. This is the only phfiycal help at prefent in the Colony, for though we have two furgeons they are both fo ill, as to difable them from helping either themfelves, or others ; one of them returns to England in the Packet, as does our *mortified soldier.*

I am, &c.

LETTER

LETTER IX.

My dear Friend,

YOU muſt not promiſe yourſelf either inſtruction or entertainment from this letter, for my ſtrength of body and mind are ſo debilitated by a ſevere fit of illneſs, that with much ado I could ſummon reſolution enough to take up my pen, or prevail on myſelf to write you a ſyllable by this opportunity, but having made a beginning (which is equal to half the taſk, I ſhall now endeavour to ſpin out what I can.

I was confined three weeks with a violent fever, ſtoneblind four days, and expecting every moment to be my laſt; indeed I moſt miraculouſly eſcaped the jaws of death: fortunately, juſt as I was taken ſick, a Phyſician arrived, to whoſe attention and ſkill I conſider myſelf principally indebted for my recovery; I am yet a poor objeꝗt, object, and being under the neceffity of having my head fhaved, tends to increafe my ghaftly figure. You will readily guefs it was very humbling and provoking for me to loofe my fine head of hair, which I always took fo much pride in, but I cannot help it, and thank God my life is preferved.

A few weeks fince arrived the Calypfo, from Bulam, with a number of difappointed adventurers who went to that Ifland; they came here in expectation of finding accommodation for a part of them during the rainy feafon, who meant afterwards to return to Bulam: but they entertained wrong notions of our Colony, when they fuppofed we had it in our power to accommodate them, for moft of our own gentlemen are obliged to fleep on fhip board, for want of houfes or lodgings on fhore.

The adventurers feem vexed at being thus defeated in their expectations, and intend to return to England in the Calypfo, when fhe fails, which will be fhortly.

Perhaps you have not heard of the Bulam expedition before, and I can give you but a very imperfect account of it, however, I will laconically tell you what I know.   A Mr.

A Mr. Dalrymple was engaged by the Directors of the Sierra Leone Company to come out as Governor of this Colony; but they difagreed from fome trifling circum-ftance, and Mr. Dalrymple feeling him-felf offended, fet on foot towards the lat-ter end of laft year) a fubfcription for forming a fettlement on the Ifland I am fpeaking of, in oppofition to the Sierra Leone Company ; A number of fpecula-tors foon affociated, fubfcribed to Mr. Dalrymple's plan, and I fancy, prema-turely fet about the completion of its ob-jects, before they had well digefted the theory, or accumulated a fufficient fund to enfure fuccefs ; be that as it may, they purchafed a fmall floop, char-tered the Calypfo and another fhip, en-gaged numbers of needy perfons, who with many of the fubfcribers, perfonally embarked in the enterprize, and placing themfelves under the direction of Mr. Dalrymple, and a few others, failed from England in April laft, and arrived at Bulam in June.

I underftand they were all novices in the arts and modes requifite for attaining their wifhed for poffeffion, which was unfortunate, for their ignorance led them into an error, that proved fatal to feveral.

Although

Although the ifland of Bulam was uninhabited, it was claimed by perfons refiding
on the adjacent Iflands, who by fome means
or other, learned the errand of the adventurers, and to prevent them from getting a
footing without confent of the proprietors,
fecretly landed a party of men on the Ifland, where they, for feveral days watched
the motions of Mr. Dalrymple's people :
between thirty and forty of whom having
difembarked and landed, (without any previous ceremony, according to the cuftom
of the country,) the natives took the firft
opportunity to catch them off their guard,
fell upon them, killed five men and one
woman, wounded two men, carried off
three or four woman and children, and
obliged the remainder to return to their
fhip.

After this Mr. Dalrymple went to the
neighbouring Ifland of Biffao, belonging
to the Portuguefe, where he, through the
medium of a merchant of that country,
became acquainted with the meafures he
fhould have adopted at firft, and having
courted the friendfhip of the native chiefs,
and made them fenfible of his peaceable
and honorable intentions, they reftored
the women and children uninjured and
gave him poffeffion of the Ifland, for fome
trifling

trifling acknowledgment I have not yet afcertained.

Mr. Dalrymple had accomplifhed this but a fhort time when he fell fick, and many of the emigrants forefeeing frightful hardfhips which they were unwilling to encounter during the prefent rains, he and they refolved to return to England, but firft to come hither for the purpofe I before mentioned.

The Ifland is not altogether abandoned, a Lieutenant Beaver of the Navy, with a few people, remain upon it.

Since their arrival here many of them have died, and the fhip is juft now very fickly.——So much for Bulam.

Now I muft fay fomething of ourfelves, which I have the heartfelt fatisfaction of telling you before hand will be more cheerful and fatisfactory than any thing I have heretofore faid.

By the laft fhip, Mr. Clarkfon received inftructions from the Directors, vefting him with more ample powers than he held before : this was much to be wifhed for, and its beneficial effects are already vifible.

Directly

Directly after getting this enlargement of authority, Mr. Clarkſon invited all the gentlemen and ladies in the Colony to dine at a meſs houſe, built for the gentlemen who came out in the Sierra Leone Packet; every one who was well enough, gladly attended to celebrate a meeting which was intended to give birth to pleaſantneſs, unanimity, and perpetual harmony; and to deface every thing to the contrary, that previouſly exiſted in the Colony: The day I am told (for being ſick at the time, I could not be there) was ſpent, as it ſhould be, with every demonſtration of ſatisfaction, by all parties, and the houſe was named *Harmony Hall*, by which name it is now, and I ſuppoſe ever will be known, while a ſtick of it ſtands: This houſe, and the one I have, are all the buildings yet finiſhed, (I mean for the Whites), but ſeveral others are about.

The Colony is growing healthier every day; moſt of the Blacks are able to turn out to work. The men are employed in the Company's ſervice, and receive two ſhillings per day wages, out of which they pay four ſhillings per week for their proviſions.

The women are occupied in attending their little gardens, and rearing poultry.
The

The natives daily grow more intimate with us, and are conftantly bringing in fruits of different kinds, but feldom any live ftock, unlefs now and then a few fowls, or perhaps a goat, which they bar-ter away for cloath, foap, or fpirits.

Every moon-light night we hear the drums of King Jemmy's town, which is fcarcely half a mile from hence. This mufic of our neighbours, for a long time after we arrived, ufed frequently to alarm the Colony; but by cuftom it has become familiar. For feveral months *King* Jemmy could not be perfuaded to come into Free Town; but at laft being prevailed upon, and relifhing his reception, he now repeats his vifits fo often, as to be very trouble-fome. Whenever he comes, a boy attends him with a pair of horfeman's piftols, loaded, and I will not be furprifed, if he does mifchief with them fome day or other for he never returns home until he has drank a fufficient quantity of rum or brandy, to kindle his favage nature for any manner of wickednefs.

The laft fhip brought out a large houfe of one hundred feet in length, which is to be erected in the vicinity of the town as an hofpital ; but the people being moftly cn the recovery, I think it would be more advifable

advifable to erect it as a ftore-houfe, and
thereby not only fave the Company's valuable property, which is juft now perifhing for want of fhelter ; but would ferve as
a repofitory for vending many goods that
are wafting on board of fhips, which would
greatly contribute to our comfort, and
which we are deprived of from not having
a proper place where they might be expofed to fale; and again, I do not think
our Blacks will fubmit to be fent to an
hofpital, therefore, the intention will be
fruftrated, however, the houfe is fo conftructed, that it can be put up or taken
down in a few hours, confequently may,
at any time hereafter, be removed ; and
we underftand feveral houfes of the fame
kind are expected in two large fhips, which
are hourly looked for.

Since the rains, we have been fadly infefted by a variety of infects, but more
particularly cockroaches and ants ; the
latter come from their nefts in fuch formidable force, as to ftrike terror where-
ever they go. You will think it ftrange,
that fuch an infignificant infect as the ant
is in England, fhould be able in another
country, to ftorm the habitations of people,
and drive out the inhabitants ; but I pledge
my veracity to you, I have known them
in

in one night, force twelve or fourteen families from their houfes, who were obliged to make ufe of fire and boiling water to deftroy them, which are the only weapons we can attack them with, that will effectually check their progrefs.

Mufquetos are not fo troublefome here as I have felt them elfewhere ; but we have a perpetual croaking of frogs and buzzings of various vermin, very difcordant and unpleafant to the ear of a perfon in perfect health, yet much more fo to thofe who are fick.

There has been feveral large ferpents killed in the Colony, but none of the overgrown fize ; Lieutenant Mathews and other authors mention, the largeft I have heard of, meafured nine feet in length.— We have been twice vifited by fome ferocious wild beaft, fuppofed to be a Tyger; the laft time it was attacked by two maftiffs of ours, who were beat off and materially injured. One of my poor domeftics, a very heavy Newfoundland dog, had his throat terribly lacerated : the other, I imagine, fought fhy, as he came off with little damage.

There are many good hunters among our Settlers, through whom we fometimes
get

get wild deer or pork; the latter is a coarfe unpleafant food; I lately had a haunch, the hide of which was full an inch and an half thick; the former is meagre, dry meat, very unlike your Englifh venifon, but fuch as it is, we are glad when it comes in our way.

Some little time ago an accident happened, one of the moft expert hunters we have, which has confiderably leffened our fupply of game; he was laying in ambufh near where he new a deer frequented; another perfon, in purfuit of the fame, paffing hard by, and hearing the ruftling of leaves, immediately fired into the thicket from whence the noife proceeded, and lodged the greater contents of his gun in the head and right fhoulder of his unfortunate rival, but, not killing him, he brought him home, two miles through the wood, on his fhoulder. Falconbridge extracted feveral of the fhot, and thinks he may recover.

Our Botanift and Mineralift have, as yet, made little proficiency in thofe branches of natural philofophy; the confufion of the Colony has retarded them as well as others; they are both Swedes, and confidered very eminent in their profeffions,

feffions. The Mineralift is about to make an excurfion into the interior country, and is very fanguine in his expectations. He has but flightly explored the country hereabouts, and been as flightly rewarded; the only fruits of his refearches are a few pieces of iron oar, richly impregnated with magnetifm, with which the mountains abound.

The Botanift is preparing a garden for experiments, and promifes himfelf much amufement and fatisfaction, when he can ftrictly attend to his bufinefs. His garden is now very forward, but it is attended with confiderable expence; however, a mere nothing, when put into the great fcale of Colonial charges, which, including fhipping, Officers' falaries, wages of labourers, and provifions, does not amount to lefs than the enormous fum of one hundred and fifty pounds per day, without naming incidental charges, fuch as prefents to natives, daily wafte and deftruction of property, &c. Thofe aggregated from the birth of the Company, to the prefent time, may at leaft be computed at 25,000l.

This is not a fuppofition of my own, for I have heard it from thofe who muft certainly

certainly be informed on the bufinefs;
but notwithftanding the Company's purfe
is fo much weakened, by folly and want
of circumfpe&ion, if the harmony and
good underftanding, at prefent exifting in
the Colony, continues, it is yet fufficiently
ftrong, by being applied with method, and
proper exertions, not only to retrieve their
loffes, and anfwer their original laudable
and magnanimous purpofes, but amply re-
quite any pecuniary motives they may
have.

Mr. Falconbridge has obtained permiffion from Mr, Clarkfon to commence his
commercial career, and had fele&ed goods
for the purpofe, but was checked by illnefs, and is dangeroufly ill at this moment.
If he recovers, his firft affay will be on the
Gold Coaft, where he anticipates fuccefs,
and often fays he hopes to cheer the de-
fpondent Dire&ors, by a valuable and un-
expe&ed cargo.

Mr. Clarkfon thinks it too early to med-
dle with trade, from the idea that it will
procraftinate the regularity and comfort of
the Colony, which he is ftrenuoufly endeavouring to eftablifh, but from my flen-
der notion of things, I humbly beg leave
to differ from him, and rather fuppofe it
would

would greatly contribute to accelerate his wifhes; at leaft it would not be the fmall-eft hindrance, or by any means interfere with our police, which to be fure will not yet bear a fcrupulous inveftigation ; however it is mending, and I dare fay, in time, our able, zealous pilot, will fteer us clear of the labyrinth which he found us entangled in.

May it be fo, is the earneft wifh of,

Your's, &c. &c.

LETTER

LETTER X.

My dear Friend,

WITHIN ten or twelve days after the date of my laſt, arrived the two ſhips that were expected. One is the York, a large veſſel of a thouſand tons (belonging to the Company), that is intended to end her days here in the character of a ſtoreſhip, for which purpoſe ſhe is admirably adapted; the other is the Samuel and Jane, likewiſe a veſſel of great burden, chartered to remain here ſix months if wanted. This veſſel arrived ſome days before the York; in her came a Mr. Wallis, to ſuperſede Falconbridge; the Directors having thought proper to annul his appointment as Commercial Agent.

That they had a right to do ſo, I will not queſtion; but methinks it developes treachery;

treachery; and I now fufpect their whole
conduct to us in England, was only a complication of hypocritical fnares, to anfwer
felfifh purpofes, which having attained,
they cared not any longer to wear the
mafk.

In their difmiffion they accufe Falconbridge of not extending their commercial
views, and wanting commercial knowledge. The latter charge may be in fome
meafure well founded, for Mr. Falconbridge was bied to phyfic, and men of per-
fpicuity would have known how unfit fuch
a perfon muft be for a merchant, indeed
he was aware of it himfelf, but it being a
place of much expected profit, (a temptation not to be withftood), he was in hopes
by application, foon to have improved the
little knowledge he had, fo as to benefit
both his employers and himfelf; but in this
they difappointed him, and were actually
the caufe of choking the attempts he might
have made.

They fhould recollect the deep deception played upon him. He left England
with independant and unlimited powers,
which were reftrained immediately on our
arrival here. Thus bridled, with the reins
in poffeffion of men, who confidered com-
merce

merce only as a fecondary view of the
Company, and who negatived every propofition of the kind Falconbridge made,
till a very fhort time before his appointment was annulled.—What was he to do?

Two days before his difmiffion came out,
he crawled from his fick bed, and, at the
moment it was delivered him, was in the
act of arranging and preparing matters for
the trading voyage I mentioned in my laft.
I am certain it proved a mortal ftab to him;
he was always addicted to drink more than
he fhould; but after this by way of me-
liorating his harrowed feelings, he kept
himfelf conftantly intoxicated; a poor, forlorn remedy you will fay; however, it anfwered his wifh, which I am convinced
was to operate as poifon, and thereby finifh
his exiftence; he fpun out his life in an-
guifh and mifery till the 19th inftant, when
without a groan he gafp'd his laft!!!

I will not be guilty of fuch meannefs
as to tell a falfhood on this occafion, by
faying I regret his death, no! I really do
not, his life had become burthenfome
to himfelf and all around him, and
his conduct to me, for more than two
years paft, was fo unkind, (not to give
a harfher term) as long fince to wean
every fpark of affection or regard I
ever

ever had for him. This I am perfuaded,
was his greateft crime; he poffeffed many
virtues, but an excellent dutiful fon, and
a truly honeft man, were confpicuous traits
in his chara&er.

I fhall now return to the arrival of the
York; in this fhip came out the Rev. Mr.
Horne and a Mr. Dawes, who is a new appointed member of council. I muft not
proceed any further till I inform you,
the Dire&ors have wholly changed their
original fyftem of government, difmounted
the old Council, and placed their political
reins in the hands of Mr. Clarkfon, who is
to be affifted by two Counfellors, one of
whom is the gentleman I juft mentioned,
the other is not yet appointed.

This new miniftry is titled, " The Governor and Council," and are charged with
the management of all civil, military, and
commercial affairs, but have no authority
whatever to interferr in ecclefiaftical matters, which are left to the guidance of Mr.
Horne or any other Minifter for the time
being.

Time will fhew whether this alteration
of politics proves propitious, as yet things
have not fallen off, but rather mended.

We

We are and have been frequently much pestered by renegade seamen, quitting ships employed in the Slave Trade, and refuging here, to the great detriment of their employers and inconveniences of the Colony. This circumstance considerably perplexes Mr. Clarkson, who, on the one hand is not only threatened with lawsuits by the masters and owners of ships, detained for want of their sailors, but is well convinced of the injury they sustain; on the other, his orders are to *protect every man,* which leaves him in an aukward situation, and at a loss what to do; however, by way of intimidation to practices of the kind, he had the following notification, (which has not availed any thing) sent to some of the neighbouring factories and stuck up in the Colony :

———————————

FREE TOWN, SIERRA LEONE,

Sept. 3*d,* 1792.

" This is to give Notice, that I will not on any account, permit Seamen, who may leave their respective Vessels, to take shelter in this Colony; and I shall give orders in future, that the Constables seize every man who cannot give a good account

count of himfelf, or whom they may fufpect to have deferted from their employ.
At the fame time I fhall be always ready
to liften to the complaints of every injured man, and fhall tranfmit their affida-
vits home to England, provided they make
application in a proper manner.

(Signed)

JOHN CLARKSON."

It is much to be lamented, however
defirable the abolition of the Slave Trade
may be, while it is fanctioned by the Englifh Government, property of individuals
in that trade fhould be harraffed and annoyed by want of order and regularity in
this Colony, or by the fanatical prejudices
of any fet of men. One fhip in particular has fuffered moft effentially, viz. the
Fifher, Clark, of Liverpool, whofe men
deferted from her in July laft, and though
fhe has had her cargo engaged ever fince,
fhe is not yet able to quit the coaft for
want of feamen; fome of whom died, and
others are now here, *employed in the Company's service.*

On the 26th, 27th, and 28th of Sep-
tember, there was an affembly of native
Chieftains here, and a Palaver was held
for

for the purpofe of afcertaining the limits
of the Company's territory. This was attended with confiderable more expence
than Falconbridge's palaver, and the confequence far lefs productive. They finifhed by curtailing the bounds, from twenty
miles fquare, (the quantity purchafed by
Captain Thompfon, and afterwards confirmed to the St George's Bay Company)
to about two miles and a quarter fronting
the fea, and running in a direct line back,
as far as the diftrict of Sierra Leone may
be, which is generally fuppofed not to
exceed five or fix miles, and three fourths
of it a barren, rocky, mountainous country, where it will be impoffible for men,
who are to earn their bread by agriculture, even to fupport themfelves; but
admitting it was all good, there is not
more than will enable the Com any to
comply with one-fifth part of their engage-
m n s to the Blacks brought from America, which proportion is now furveying
for t em.

This circumftance, I am perfuaded, will
hereafter lead to much difcontent and uneafinefs among the fettlers, and, if I do
not foothfay wrongly, will fhackle thofe
gentlemen who have been the inftruments
of removing them with fuch difgrace as
they will not eafily expunge.

When

When the Palaver was ended, and Naimbaca (who prefided a it on the part of the natives) was about to return to Ro-bana. Mr. Clarkfon, by way of amufing and complimenting the King, took him in a boat with fix oarsmen and a cockfwain, who rowed them through the fleet in the harbour, confifting of fix or feven fail; each veffel, as they paffed, faluted them with feveral guns, till they came to the Harpy, when they were not noticed by the fmalleft token of refpect, on the contrary, Captain Wilfon called to Mr. Clark-fon and told him he had a few words to fay to him; Mr. Clarkfon replied, if they were not of much confequence he wifhed to be excufed juft then, but upon Wil-fon's affuring him they were of fome importance, the Governor complied with his requeft and went on board: Captain Wilfon then faid, he was much offended that Mr. Clarkfon fhould take a boat's crew from his fhip, and a cockfwain from another; till that moment Mr. Clark-fon had not obferved fuch to be the cafe, and affured Captain Wilfon it was done inadvertently, without the flighteft intention of giving offence. This acknowledgment was not enough for Captain Wilfon, and his temper being irritated, he ufed fome very indifcreet expreffions to Mr. Clark-

fon,

fon, fuch as telling him : " Damn me, Sir,
if ever you fhall have another boat's crew
from my fhip, unlefs you have a cockfwain
alfo," &c. &c. The governor was hurt
at fuch language and returned to his boat;
King Naimbana enquired of him why
that fhip did not fire ? he anfwered " Mrs.
Wilfon is fick, and the captain does not
like to difturb her with the noife."

The King then embarked on board the
Lapwing Cutter, ard went home: When
he was gone, and the Colony clear of all
the Chiefs, Mr. Clarkfon fent a meffage
to Captain Wilfon, defiring him to make
an apology for his unhandfome behaviour,
or he (Mr. Clarkfon) would be under the
neceffity of taking fteps very repugnant
to his inclination. Wilfon pofitively refufed, and continuing obftinate two days,
(wholly engroffed with meffages and anfwers, to and fro), Mr. Clarkfon, although
a man of humility and condefcenfion, unwilling to brook fo grofs an infult, fummoned every gentleman in the Colony to
meet him on board the Amy; and when
they were collected, wrote a letter, fum-
moning Captain Wilfon: which fummons
being difobeyed, he appealed to the affembly, who unanimoufly determined, the
delinquent fhould be difmiffed from command

mand of the Harpy; in consequence whereof, his dismission, signed by the Governor and Mr. Dawes, was sent immediately.

When the boat that carried it, came under the Harpy's stern, (being a little after eight at night,) she was hailed, and asked whither she was bound? " To the Harpy, with a letter for Captain Wilson," answered the bearer; " I am desired to inform you, no boat will be permitted to come along side at such an improper hour; and, if you proceed a boat's length further, Captain Wilson's orders are to fire on you" replied a voice from the Harpy: these threats not intimidating the boat's crew, two muskets were actually fired on them, but did no mischief; and reaching the ship before another fire, the undaunted messenger attempted to ascend the gangway, but was prevented by the ship's company, who cut away the gangway ropes, and beat him off with cutlasses, sticks, &c.

Captain Wilson having learned the purport of this letter, from some person who afterwards went on board, declared he would not be removed from his ship with life, and he would blow out that man's brains, who dared attempt to enforce him!

This

This boisterous disposition subsided by
the following day, when his dismission,
with minutes of every gentleman's opinion
who had been at the meeting over night,
were sent him   He then persisted that he
would not *tamely* leave his ship, but if
any person, authorised, forcibly attempted
to take him out, he would make no un-
lawful resistance.   Mr. Dawes volunteered
this duty, went on board, and after, in
vain, perfuading Wilson not to put him
to the unpleasant task of using violence,
he took him by the collar, and *gently* led
him over the ship's side.   When descend-
ing into the boat, he called to his Officers and men, " Observe! I am forced
out of my ship."   He was then conducted
to the York, where he was informed his
residence would be until an opportunity
offered to fend him to England.

This fracas being thus quieted, perfect
harmony otherwise subsisting among us,
and Mr. Clarkson having some idea of
returning to Europe, wished before hand,
to furnish Mr. Dawes with a trial of his
influence among the Blacks, and individual management of the Colony; and
judging a trip to sea, for a few weeks,
would be the best means of affording
such an opportunity, he sailed in the
Amy

Amy on the 2d of October, in company with a fmall brig of the Sierra Leone Company's, then bound home to England; but in which Mr. and Mrs. Wilfon could not take their paffage, the accommodations being previoufly difpofed of.

When Mr. Clarkfon failed, he defired Captain Wilfon might be informed, he was not to confider himfelf a prifoner, but at liberty to conduct himfelf as he pleafed, and vifit any where he liked, except the *Harpy*, which fhip he was ftrictly prohibited from putting his foot on board.

In about three weeks Mr. Clarkfon returned; a multiplicity of complaints were then poured into him by the Settlers, againft Mr. Dawes, whofe auftere, referved conduct (fo reverfe to the fweet manners of the other, they could not poffibly relifh, and confequently all hopes or expectations of the latter gaining popularity, proved abortive. It may not be *mal-a-propos* to mention here, that Mr. Dawes is a fubaltern of Marines; that the prejudices of a rigid military education has been heightened by his having ferved, fome time at Botany Bay, where, no doubt, it is neceffary for gentlemen to obferve an awful feverity in their looks and actions;

tions; but fuch behaviour, however fuitable for a Colony formed wholl of Convicts. and governed by the i: n rod of
defpotifm, fhould be fcrupluoufly guarded
again* in one like this, whofe *basis is Liberty and Equality,* and whofe Police is
dependant, in great meafure, if not altogether, on the whimfical difpofition of
an ignorant populace, which can only be
advantageoufly tempered by placidnefs and
moderation.

The Directors having ordered home the
Harpy, when fhe could be fpared from
the Colony, Mr. Clarkfon, on his return,
defired fhe might be expeditioufly fitted
for fea, and on the 28th of laft month,
being Sunday, and moft of the Colony
pioufly engaged, Captain Wilfon, knowing fhe was nearly ready, availed himfelf
of the chance, and through the means of
her boat, that came under pretence of
giving him an airing, replaced himfelf, by
confent of his Officers and crew, in command of his fhip, and immediately after
divine fervice, Mr. Clarkfon received the
following letter from him.

November 18, 1792.

SIR,

I apprehend it is needlefs to inform you I have taken poffeffion of the Harpy, and mean, in defiance of all oppofition, to carry her to England.

As I fhould be very forry to be exceeded in politenefs on this occafion,* I write this to afk your commands for London, intending to fail immediately ; neverthelefs, Sir, if within an hour I receive an anfwer, affuring me of your pacific intentions, figned by *yourfelf* and *Mr. Dawes*, I will wait your orders.

Take care, Sir, how you attempt any thing like force ; if blood is fhed, be it upon your head. Wifhing you more prudence, and better advifers,

I remain, Sir,

Your moft humble Servant,

T. H. WILSON.

John Clarkfon, Efq. &c. &c.

This

* Mr. Clarkfon had wrote a day or two before this to Mrs. Wilfon, offering *her* a paffage in the Harpy, and at the fame time informing Captain Wilfon, fhe was to fail in a few days, if he wifhed to write.

This was a ſtep ſo unlooked for, that it puzzled the Governor and Council how to conduct themſelves: after ſome deliberation, they determined not to anſwer Captain Wilſon's letter, and the time he limited having elapſed, we ſaw the Harpy under the guns of the York, and under the guns of the Battery, get under way, and triumphantly ſail off.

Various opinions prevailed reſpecting the propriety of Captain Wilſon's repoſſeſſing himſelf of the Harpy : ſome ſaid it was an act of piracy, and they were certain he would never take her to England; but others judged leſs harſhly, with whom I join; and, from my knowledge of Captain Wilſon, feel myſelf authoriſed to ſay, he poſſeſſes too great a ſhare of pride, and too high a ſenſe of honor, to ſhipwreck his character on the rock of infamy—but at the ſame time will not aver him inerrable; on the contrary, think his behaviour to Mr. Clarkſon monſtrous diſreſpectful and inconſiſtent, which, without doubt, he was betrayed into by warmth of temper, and too lofty, but wrong notions of punctilio's.

I have been particularly obliged to Captain Wilſon, therefore it would be truly ungenerous, nay, the blackeſt ingratitude

in

in me, mifchievoufly, to hint at any thing prejudicial to him, and muft beg you not to fuppofe I have touched upon the fub-ject by way of affailing his character; con-fidering it a circumftance of importance, I could not pafs it over in filence.*

On the 2d inftant arrived the Felicity from England. I mention the arrival of this veffel, becaufe fhe was expected to bring a number of ufeful ftores for the Colony, in place of which her cargo con-fifted principally of *garden watering pots*.

In her way out fhe ftopped at Gambia, and took in feveral head of cattle, whereby we are now and then indulged with roaft beef, the firft we have had fince our ar-rival, for the inhabitants, here-abouts, are too indolent to attend to rearing domeftic quadrupeds of any kind.—King Naimbana has two or three very fat beeves; and I think there may be as many more at Bance Ifland; but, before the Felicity arrived, I can venture to fay, thofe were all in this part of the country, unlefs I include a couple of milch cows, and a bull brought out from England by the York, which, from

---

* Should this Narrative meet the eye of Captain Wilfon, I truft he will do me the juftice to fay, I have not wandered from the broadway of truth,

from the inimical climate, died in a very
fhort time. Thefe brought from Gambia
are thin, the flefh dark and coarfe, and
only the name of beef as a recommen-
dation. Mutton and goat's flefh are the
moft preferable in their kinds ; indeed,
the former, though not overloaded with
fat, I think nearly as fweet as our Englifh
mutton, but the little we get of them, come
chiefly from the interior country.

About the latter end of October, the
rains began to diminifh ; and for a month
paft have entirely ceafed : they are fucceeded by denfe, difagreeable, and unwholefome fogs, which are fuppofed will
continue near a month longer. Thefe
are termed fmoaks, and confidered more
unhealthy than the worft rains, but we cannot fay fo from experience, for the Colony
is healthier juft now, than it has been fince
the beginning of May; yet a few deaths
happen now and then : among thofe who
lately died was Mr. Nordenfchold, the
Mineralift, who was taken ill on the expedition I noticed in my laft, he was
then about to make, and forced to return
without acquiring any fatisfaction for his
journey, which was attended not only with
innumerable difadvantages from the time
of year, but with many other impediments
he did not forefee or expect.

The

The lofs cf him is much to be regreted, for he was an enterprifing clever man, and no doubt, had he lived, would have procured a vaft deal of ufeful informa·tion.

The Governor and Council have at laft thought it advifable to embark in Agriculture, and have purchafed a fmall track of land on the oppofite (Bullom) fhore.—This new undertaking is placed under the management of a man, who was fome time an Overfeer in Dominica, and who was a *Member of the firft Council:* it is called *Clarkson's Plantation,* and from the richnefs and apparent fertility of the foil, much advantage may be looked for, provided no difagreement arifes with the natives, and a fufficient number of fteady labourers can be obtained; but being in its infancy, all we can do at prefent is to wifh it fuccefs, which time muft determine.

Three or four new houfes are now erected, and moft of the gentlemen are comfortably lodged; there is a retail fhop opened in the Colony, from whence we are furnifhed with fuch goods as the Directors have fent out, moft of which are not only badly adapted for a warm climate, but wretchedly bad in their kind.

We

We have little gold or filver among
us ; that want is fubftituted by paper
notes, from five dollars down to fix-pence,
figned by the Governor or Mr. Dawes.——
The credit of this medium is eftablifhed
by giving bills of exchange, to the holders,
upon the Directors, at a trifle more than
eleven per cent. difcount, which is only
the difference between fterling and currency, a guinea b ing nominally twenty-
three fhillings and four-pence here ; it is
taken in payment for goods at the Company's ftore, and its reputation is now fo
good, that the neighbouring Factories and
cafual Traders receive it for what our Settlers purchafe for them.

Mr. Clarkfon is fo convinced the Company have been fadly impofed upon, that
a few weeks ago he wrote a circular letter
to the gentlemen of the Colony, acquainting them with his intention of failing for
England very quickly,——requefting their
opinion of the various goods that came
under their notice,——their general ideas
as to the wants of the Colony, and their
advice how to prevent abufes being practifed on the Company in future.

I faw part of a letter from one gentleman in anfwer, wherein he fays,——" You
have done me the honor of afking my advice,

vice how to prevent abuſes being practiſed on the Company in future ? In anſwer to this I ſhall only ſay, it would be the height of preſumption in me to offer an opinion on the ſubject, being perſuaded your own penetration and diſcernment is ſufficient to diſcover a remedy, without the aſſiſtance of any one ; and if the Directors will attend to your advice upon this, as well as every other circumſtance reſpecting the Colony, I am ſure they will find their advantage in it."

Had my opinion been aſked, I ſhould have ſaid, " let the Directors ſhake off a parcel of hypocritical puritans, they have about them, who, under the cloak of religion, are ſucking out the very vitals of the Company ; let them employ men converſant in trade, acquainted with the coaſt of Africa, and whoſe *religious tenets have never been noticed* ; under this deſcription they will find perſons of ſound morals, fit to be intruſted, but they will ever be ſubject to impoſitions, while they employ a pack of canting paraſites, who have juſt cunning enough to deceive them."

We are in great tribulation about Mr. Clarkſon's going away, for Mr. Dawes is almoſt univerſally diſliked, and more than

probable,

probable, anarchy and difcord will again return, in full force among us, when the management of things are left to him alone; however, it is wrong to anticipate misfortunes, and our Governor has made every arrangement in his power to prevent intruders of this kind.

The Surveyor has affured him, the Blacks fhall have the proportion of land now furveying for them, in a fortnight at fartheft. Every one has pledged himfelf to ufe his utmoft efforts to preferve harmony and order during Mr. Clarkfon's abfence, which we expect will be five or fix months ; and to infure Mr. Dawes the good will of King Naimbana, he has been allowed to make the King a very confiderable prefent *out of the Company's Property.*

Adieu,

Your's, &c.

JOURNAL.

JOURNAL.

TWO days ago Mr. Clarkſon ſailed; his departure operated more powerfully and generally upon people's feelings, than all the deaths we have had in the Colony; ſeveral gentlemen accompanied him two or three leagues to ſea, and returned the ſame night.

Jan. 2d. The Surveyor has ſtopped ſurveying the lots of land for the Settlers, although he aſſured Mr. Clarkſon, they ſhould have them in a fortnight. His attention is now taken up with fortification, which ſeems to be the hobby-horſe of Mr. Dawes, and a large Fort is planed out upon a hill, about half a mile from the water ſide.

King Jemmy came to ſee me this day; he aſked what was the reaſon Mr. Clarkſon did not call upon him before he ſailed, and ſaid he did not ſuppoſe Mr. Clarkſon would have left the country without coming to ſee him; his cheek was furrowed with tears as he ſpoke; I did not imagine he had ſo much ſenſibility.

There

'There was a very heavy tornado laft night, an unufual thing at this time of the year; the roof of my houfe has become fo dry, that the rain had free accefs through, and I got thoroughly wet.

5th. A remarkable fine ox, (fent as a prefent to the Colony, by King Naimbana) was killed this day, I never faw fatter meat in my life; our acting governor, (notwithftanding it was a prefent) had it fold at 4d per pound. I fuppofe he has done this to fhew us he intends being an œconomift, and thereby reimburfe the Company's heavy loffes; but that will require more fat oxen than he will be able to procure in this part of Africa for fome years. This is not the only inftance of his œconomy, or I fhould fay, parfimony, for a few days after Falconbridge died, he came and demanded of me his uniform coat, fword, gun, piftols, and a few other prefents that the Directors had made him, which I gave up, they being of no ufe to me; he alfo engroffes all the *Yams, Pumpkins, Turtle,* and almoft every kind of provifions in the neighbourhood, and has them retailed from the Company's ftore at an enormous advance, when turtle is killed he fends his own fervant to take an account of the weight, left the butcher

fhould

fhould embezzle a few pounds; but I
doubt after all, he will verify the trite
proverb, " penny wife and pound foolifh,"
for I have heard it remarked by a Gentleman of information, that the new Fort,
if finifhed on the plan propofed, will coft
20,000l.

7th. This day another plantation was be
gan at Savoy Point, about half a mile from
hence, which is intended for the cultivation
of cotton, whether it fucceeds or not,
clearing the wood about the town will certainly be conducive to health.

The manager of Clarkfon's plantation
complains that moft of his gramattos or labourers have left him to attend the cry or
funeral ceremony of one of their brethren,
who lately died by the wound of a fhark;
it is uncertain how long the cry will laft.

9th. Came down from Bance Ifland,
the Duke of Buccleugh, bound for Jamaica, with upwards of three hundred
flaves. Yefterday arrived two fhips, one
an American, the other a Frenchman;
they have plenty of provifions on board,
which the Colony is greatly in want of.
Mr. Dawes called on moft of the gentlemen to requeft they would not purchafe
any,

any, faying he intends buying what is wanted by wholefale, and will retail it to them at a *small advance*; fuch a propofal would have come better from a Jew pedlar, than from the Governor of Sierra Leone, or a Lieutenant of Marines.

11th. The Duke of Buccleugh failed yefterday, and the Frenchman this day. I underftand Mr. Dawes has purchafed fome articles of provifion from the Frenchman, who would have nothing but flaves in return, and for the fake of accommodation, Mr. Dawes gave him an order on Mr. Rennieu, who pays him in flaves. I think if this is not, it borders on an infringement of the Act of Parliament, for incorporating the Company, which fays; " the Company fhall not, through the medium of their fervants, or otherwife, directly, or indirectly, traffic in flaves." It feems as if Providence frowns on this purchafe, for an unufual high tide carried away part of the provifions after they were landed.

A fmall coafting cutter of the Company's called the Providence, arrived this day from the Turtle iflands, about fifteen leagues to leeward; fhe brought eight goats, four fheep, and twenty-one turtle; fixteen

fixteen of the latter died fince twelve
o'clock, which has difconcerted the Governor very much; but I am told he has made
a *calculation*, and thinks, if he can fell the
other five, at *four-pence per pound*, it will
be yet a *saving voyage*.

Between eleven and twelve o'clock laft
night, the Colony was alarmed by the
report of guns, beating of drums, and
fhrill fhoutings of our neighbours at
King Jemmy's town.—Mr. Dawes affem-
bled all the men, and had arms and ammunition given them, from a fuppofition
that the natives meant to attack us—but
it turned out to be a groundlefs alarm, and
is fufpected to have been a contrivance
of fome ill-difpofed perfons to get the
Settlers armed.

King Jemmy and Signior Domingo
being informed of this, came to-day to
enquire why their *good faith* was mif-
trufted; they dined with Mr. Dawes,
and after dinner King Jemmy paid me
a vifit; he feemed much offended, and
faid it was very foolifh to fuppofe he
would make war without a caufe—if he
had a Palaver with the Colony, he would
firft come and talk it over, and if it could
not be fettled in that way, and he was
forced

forced to make war, he would give us timely notice, that we might defend ourfelves, but it was the cuftom of his country to compromife difputes amicably, and never to engage in war till there was no other alternative, or words to the fame effect.—The former affertion, I believe, is not untrue, and his behaviour to the firft Settlers is an example; in that difpute, he gave them three days notice of his intention to drive them off, and burn their town;—with regard to the latter, I have frequently heard wars were common among the natives for the purpofe of obtaining flaves; fuch may have been the practice, but I have enquired of feveral Chiefs, who pofitively deny it; and I am certain, fince my firft acquaintance in this part of the world, none of thofe predatory wars have happened hereabouts, notwithftanding upwards of two thoufand flaves have been fhipped and fent to the Weft Indies, from this river, within thefe laft twelve months.

15th. Arrived a Cutter belonging to Bance Ifland, from the Ifles de Lofs. A Mr. M'Auley, Member of Council, and the Reverend Mr. Gilbert, came paffengers in her. Thefe gentlemen came from England to the River Gambia, in the

Sierra

Sierra Leone Packet, where they left her to take in cattle for the Colony. The Settlers are highly pleafed at Mr. Gilbert's return; indeed every one muft rejoice in the fociety of fo amiable a man.

I have net heard any thing of Mr. M'Auley, except his lately being an Overfeer upon an eftate in Jamaica: It is not to be queftioned that the prejudices of fuch an education muft imprefs him with fentiments favorable to the Slave Trade, and confequently I fhould not fuppofe him qualified for a Member of Adminiftration in a Colony moftly formed of *Blacks*, founded on principles of *freedom*, and for the *express purpose* of abolifhing the Slave Trade.

16th. I heard this morning there was another alarm laft night, but as groundlefs as the laft. Seven or eight canoes full of natives, paffing the fettlement on their way to King Jemmy's, hooping and hallooing as they went, ftirred up unneceffary fears in the minds of the Settlers, who floc'ed to Mr. Dawes, requefting he would furnifh them with ammunition, which (not thinking requifite he refufed, and they returned home greatly diffatisfied.

I learn

I learn thofe people are come down to make one of their periodical Sacrifices to the *Devil*—I fhould like to witnefs the ceremony, but ftrangers (particularly whites) are not admiffible; it will be performed between Free Town and King Jemmy's, on the fide of a fmall brook, under a clufter of large trees.

The weather is particularly fine at prefent—the fogs or fmoaks are moftly difpelled, a falubrious fea breeze fans us daily, and agreeably tempers the burning fun.

17th. We are prodigioufly diftreffed to underftand King Naimbana is fo dangeroufly ill, that his death is hourly looked for:—Mr. Dawes, Mr. Gilbert, the Phyfician, and fome others, went up to vifit him this morning; his death will certainly inconvenience the colony very much.

Laft night arrived the Lapwing cutter from the river Carimanca, (twelve or thirteen leagues from hence) with a load of Camwood, ivory, and rice—the Company have a fmall factory there, under the direction of a free mulatto-man, but the trade is yet very trifling, not nearly equal to the charges attending it.

That

That river produces the largeſt and fineſt oyſters I ever eat—not ſuch as are in common hereabouts, generated on the mangrove tree, and rocks, but genuine bed oyſters—I have been fortunate enough to get a ſupply of them ſeveral times.

The Settlers, having now a number of ſmall boats, are able to furniſh the Colony with abundance of capital fiſh, and they have ſuch plenty of fowls, that the gentlemen get what they require; but propagation of the feathered ſpecies, is conſiderably protracted by the multitude of enemies they have here, viz. ſnakes, rats, wild cats, armadillas,* ants, &c.——The moſt formidable of all theſe are the ants—in the dead hour of night, they come in ſwarms, and attack the helpleſs chickens, while rooſting under the mother's wing, who is ſcarcely able to defend herſelf.—I have had four or five killed in a night by them; and ſo prying and aſſiduous are they after their prey, that I have known them diſcover two doves, which were hanging in a cage up one pair of ſtairs, whom they not only killed, but carried off every morſel, except the feathers, before morning.

19th.

* A kind of ſcaly lizzard.

19th. Mr. Dawes and two or three
other gentlemen went to Bunch river
this morning to vifit Pa Bunkie, who
fome people imagine will fucceed King
Naimbana ; they took a prefent, or as it
is termed, Dafh, for this Chieftain, by far
richer than any yet made, King Naimbana, or any other Chief.

Returning in the evening, they ftoped at
Signior Domingo's, where they expected
to have feen a late favourite woman of
King Jemmy's drink the red water, for
fufpicion of witchcraft, but their curiofity
was difappointed by the ceremony being
performed in an inland town ; however
they were informed the woman had drank
the water, and recovered, and in confequence, Jemmy, by the cuftoms of
his country, is obliged either to pay the
woman's parents, a flave, or the value
of one in goods.

At half paft twelve o'clock, P. M. a
fpark from the Kitchen fire, kindled in
the roof of my houfe, and before water
could be procured, communicated itfelf
in all directions : In a few moments the
roof fell in, and in lefs then fifteen minutes, the whole building was confumed ;
but by the extraordinary exertions of fome
labourers

labourers who were working hard by, moſt of my cloaths and furniture were ſaved, ſo that my loſs is trifling. I ſuppoſe (from a curſory view of what has eſcaped), not above 50l. As luck would have it, I moved my lodgings ſome days ago, and only ſtayed in the thatched houſe du·ing the day, intending to leave it entirely, when another room was finiſhed in the houſe where I now am, which will be the caſe ſhortly; indeed, it is already ſo forward, that I have aſked a party of two and twenty to dine with me the day after to-morrow, on an *extraordinary occaſion*, therefore I cannot complain of *wanting shelter*.

20th. I have been informed, that Pa Bunkie was adviſed by his Palaver-Man, not to accept the great *dash*, which Mr. Dawes carried him yeſterday; and that this Palaver *Gentleman* made uſe of the following, or fimilar language, to diſſuade him from taking it :

" Father—theſe people have been here twelve moons now, have they ever taken the ſlighteſt notice of you, by inviting you to their camp,* or making you the ſmalleſt preſent heretofore ?—No, Father !

* The name given *Free Town* by the Natives.

Father!— And what makes them thus suddenly over generous to you ?—Becaufe they think your fervices will foon be requifite for them. Do not you know white men well enough, to be convinced they never give away their money without expecting it returned many fold ?— Cannot you fee the drift of this profufe, unlooked for, and unafked for prefent ? Let me warn you againft taking it—for be affured, however difinterefted and friendly they appear at this moment, they are aiming at fome felfifh purpofes, and although they may not difcover what their wifhes are immediately — before twelve moons more you will know them."— Bunkie replied, " I know they want fomething, neverthelefs I'll take the *dash*— it refts with me, whether to comply with any requeft they make or not. I fhall not confider the prefent, by any means binding on me."

Mr. Gilbert and Mr. Horne went up this afternoon to Signior Domingo's, where Mr. Horne preached a fermon to a congregation of natives. How prepofterous ! Is it poffible a fenfible man, like Mr. Horne, can fuppofe it in his power to imprint notions of Chriftianity, or any fort of inftruction, upon the minds of people,

people, through the bare medium of a
language they do not underftand? He
might as well expect holding a can-
dle to the eyes of a blind man, or ex-
pofing him to the fun, would reclaim his
fight! The defire of fpreading Chriftian
knowledge through this ignorant land, is
queftionlefs, moft praife worthy, but it
will require patience and time to effect
it.

21ft. Laft night arrived the Naffau,
(Morley) from Briftol, but laft from the
Ifles de Lofs: Captain Morley this day
added to the number at our convivial
gala: I was highly complimented for the
elegance, variety, and richnefs of my
dinner, which, without doubt was fuperb,
confidering where we are ; we had three
removes, from fix and twenty to thirty
difhes each; befides an admirable defert,
confifting of a variety of European and
tropical fruit, the whole of which was gar-
nifhed with comfort and pleafantry.

24th. On Sunday laft, notice was given
that Mr. Horne, or Mr. Gilbert would
perform divine fervice, in future, every
morning and evening ; and every one is
defired to attend. I am of opinion the
morning fervice is fuperfluous.—Why?
For

For many reafons, and I will here enu‑
merate three or four.

Among the Black Settlers are feven re‑
ligious fects, and each fect has one or more
preachers attached to it, who alternately
preach throughout the whole night; indeed,
I never met with, heard, or read of, any
fet of people obferving the fame appear‑
ance of godlinefs; for I do not remem‑
ber, fince they firft landed here, my ever
awaking (and I have awoke at every hour
of the night, without hearing preachings
from fome quarter or other.

Now, thofe people being fo religioufly
bent, I think it unneceffary, or, as I firft
faid, fuperfluous, that they fhould be con‑
vened every morning; becaufe the primeft
part of the day, for exercifing their worldly
vocations, i occupied thereby; the vicious
and lazy (and fome fuch will creep into
every fociety), are furnifhed with the plea
of being at church; an excufe, I am told,
many already make, after fkulking an hour
or two beyond the cuftomary and proper
time, when they have not been within a
church door; and it detains the mafs of
labourers an hour every day, which, loft
time, cofts the Company at the rate of
1300l. per annum.

Vice

Vice and lazinefs fu ·ly ought not to be protected by Religion any where; but they fhould be more efpecially difcountenanced in a new col ny, where fuccefs greatly depends on induftry.

This day I dined on board the Naffau, in company with Mr. Rennieu, and fome gentlemen of the Colony.

Rennieu fays, an old man named *Congo Bolokelly*, is on his way from the interior country to fucceed King Naimbana; and fuch great pains has been taken to imprefs him with an unfavourable opinion of our Colony, that he is determined the Company fhall re-purchafe their land, or he will do every thing in his power to perplex and annoy us.

Mr. Dawes met with a circumftance very galling to him this forenoon. He had in contemplation to palifade a piece of ground, for an immediate afylum, in cafe the natives fhould take it in their heads to attack us.

The fpot fixed upon, unfortunately took in part of a lot occupied by one of the Settlers, which, Mr. Dawes, confcious of his unpopularity, did not wifh to encroach upon,

upon, without obtaining permiffion, although the Settlers only hold their prefent Town lots as a temporary accommodation, until their permanent ones are furveyed.

He called on the tenant and took him out to explain what he wanted; many people in the neighbourhood having previoufly heard of Mr. Dawes's intentions, affenbled ab ut him, who declared they would not fuffer an inch more ground to be enclofed, upon any pretence whatever, before their t.wn and c untry lots were given them, and moft folemnly protefted they would deftroy every fence which might be erected till fuch time.

Mr. Dawes endeavoured to perfuade them by argument, what he wanted to do, was for their protection; but they were deaf to every th ng he faid, and gave him language in return which he could not ftomach: He told them if he had ima ined they would have treated him with fo much indignity, he fhould not have come among them: and if they continued to behave in the fame way, he would certai ly leave them as early as he could. To this, with ne voice. they exclaimed, "Go! go! go! we do not w nt you here, we cannot get a worfe after you."

you." He was fo difgufted at this, that he turned his back and walked off. It was directly before my door, therefore I witneffed the whole, and could not help feeling for the *Governor*, who was feemed dreadfully mortified and out of temper.

Feb. 3. Nothing worth recording for thefe ten days paft ; yefterday the manager of Clarkfon's plantation came over from Bull m ; he has had a fericus quarrel with the natives, but *reafon* was determined on his fide. His advances in cultivation. I underftand are very flow; for he is not able to keep any number of labourers together, more than a month at a time ; it is cuftomary to pay them every moon, and when they get their wages, like our Englifh tars, they quit work while they have money.

The Sierra Leone Packet arrived from Gambia this day, with thirty head of cattle ; I have not learned what her European cargo confifts of, but it is faid to be very trifling.

7th. Since the departure of Mr. Clarkfon a number of fubtle ungentlemanlike attempts have been made, to finge his reputation, in the opinion of the people, and to warp away their affections from him :
which

which as yet have proved unfuccefsful;
but I never heard of fo unmanly, unprin-
cipled, and diabolical an affault on any
one's chara&er, as was laft night made on
his. The Settlers were fummoned to meet
Mr. Dawes and the Surveyor in the
evening; and being colle&ed, they were
informed their permanent *Town Lots*
were furveyed and ready for them, and
they muft relinquifh thofe they at prefent occupy, immediately; to this they
replied, " when placed on the lots we at
prefent occupy, we were informed, they
were merely for our temporary accommodation, and we promifed, when the plan of
the town was fixed upon and furveyed we
would remove, but we were affured no
public or other buildings would be ere&ed
between our lots and the fea; now, in place
of this, the fea fhore is lined with buildings, therefore, your promife being broken,
we confider ours cancelled, and will not
remove unlefs the new lots are run from
the water's edge, and we indifcriminately,
partake of them. Mr. Clarkfon promifed
in Nova Scotia that no diftin&ion fhould
be made here between us and white men;
we now claim this promife, we are free
Britifh fubje&s, and expe& to be treated
as fuch; we will not tamely fubmit to be
trampled on any longer. Why are not
                                        our

our country allotments of land furveyed!
Why are not all the Company's promifes
to us fulfilled ? We have a high regard and
refpe&t for Mr. Clarkfon, and firmly believe he would not have left us, without
feeing every promife he made performed;
if gentlemen here had not given him the
ftrongeft affurances they fhould be complied with immediately." In anfwer, they
were told, " that it was not uncommon for
Mr. Clarkfon to make prodigal and extraordinary promifes without thinking of them
afterwards, that the great advantages he
held out to them in Nova Scotia he was in
no fhape authorifed by the Sierra Leone
Company to make ; they all came from
himfelf merely to feduce them here; and
he never had an idea of fulfilling of them,
nay, he had it not in his power, and more
than probable *was drunk* when he made
them." Here they groaned and murmured,
but faid " they believed Mr. Clarkfon to
be a man of honor, and that he never
made any promife to them but fuch as he
was authorifed by the Company to make."
The altercation now ended; I have had it
nearly in the fame language from more
than a dozen people who were at the meeting.

The blacks feem vaftly alarmed and uneafy, nothing elfe is fpoken of all this
day,

day, and I underſtand they have determined to ſend two deputies to the Court
of Directors to know from them what
footing they are on, and what were the promiſes Mr. Clarkſon was authoriſed to make
them; indeed, it is not to be wondered at,
for no other concluſion can be formed from
ſuch baſe inſinuations, but that a wiſh ex-
iſts *somewhere* to do them juſtice.

12th. We had reaſon to think, for ſome
days paſt, King Naimbana was dead, but
had no certainty of it until this morning; nor do we exactly know, when he
died, but it is ſuppoſed ſeveral days ago.
The country cuſtom is to keep a great
man's death ſecret ſome time; his coffin
(the firſt in all probability any of his family
ever had) is making here, and will be ſent
up to Robana this evening.

14th. Yeſterday being the anniverſary
of the Harpy's arrival, a few celebrated
it by dining at a houſe of a late member of Council; who came out in her; I
think it would have been more *a-propos* to
have faſted and mourned on the occaſion.
The day was cloudy, accompanied with a
a rumbling thunder and ſpitting rain,* as
                                        if

* A circumſtance rarely known at this ſeaſon.

if the heavens *were groaning and weeping at the recollection.* It was intended to have fired minute guns in compliment to the remains of Naimbana, which would have been very timely, but that ceremony was postponed until this day, when it was performed.

LETTER XI.

February 15th, 1793.

My dear Madam,

THE Good Intent, Captain Buckle, affords me an opportunity of sending you the foregoing Journal, which I fear you will think very infipid, but every day produces fuch a famenefs that really there is not fubject for high feafoning, even a common epiftle, and you will allow journalizing ftill more difficult; however, to avoid tautological writing, as much as poffible, I fkiped over feveral days at a time, which of courfe you will have obferved, but after all, it is fo dry, that I am almoft afhamed to fend it you, and am determined in future to have recourfe to my old epiftolary mode.

My

My dinner on the 21ſt of January will ſomewhat puzzle you at firſt, and leaſt you may not at once hit upon what occaſioned it, I muſt acquaint you I have changed the name of Falconbridge for one a little *shorter*, under which I beg to ſubſcribe myſelf,

Your's ſincerely, &c. &c.

LETTER

LETTER XII.

My dear Madam,

I Finifhed my laft by hinting that I had once more enlifted under the banners of Hymen, but made no apology for my haftinefs; or, in other words, for deviating from the ufual cuftom of twelve months *widowhood*. To be plain, I did not make any, becaufe I thought it unneceffary. Narrow minds may cenfure me, and perhaps the powerful influence of habit, might operate againft me in your opinion, before you reflected upon my fituation, or well digefted the many circum-ftances which plead in my favour; but having done this, I am miftaken indeed, if your heart is not too expanded to fully me with reproach afterwards. My own confcience acquits me from having acted wrong; next to that, I wifh for the appro-bation of my friends, and after them, the charitable conftruction of the world. I know you wifh me happy, and no woman can be more fo than I am at prefent, with every expectation of a continuance.

I muft

I muſt now proceed to give you a ſum.
mary view of occurrences ſince the fif.
teenth of February.

The firſt thing I ſhall mention is the
univerſal diſcontent which has prevailed
among the Settlers ever ſince the altercation they had with Mr. Dawes and the Surveyor on the 7th of February, and it
muſt be confeſſed by every candid perſon,
their murmurs are not excited without
cauſe.

To give you an idea of what their complaints are, I ſhall ſtate the outlines of a
petition which they intend ſending to the
Court of Directors by two Deputies elected
about the middle of March, who, for want
of an opportunity, have not yet ſailed,
but are juſt on the eve of embarking in
the Amy, for England. I have not only
ſeen the petition, but have a copy of it
verbatim.

It firſt of all ſtates, " That the Petitioners are ſenſible of, and thankful for the
good intended by ſending them from Nova Scotia to this country, and in return
aſſure the Directors, they are well inclined
to aſſiſt the Company's views, all in their
power.

" That

" That they are grieved beyond ex-
preffion to be forced to complain of hard-
fhi s and oppreffions loaded on them by
the managers of the Colony, which they
are perfuaded the Directors are ignorant
of.

" That the promifes made by the Company's Agents, in Nova Scotia, were preferable to any ever held out to them before,
and trufting the performance of them, with
the Almighty's affiftance, and their own induftry, would better their condition, induced them to emigrate here. That none
of thofe promifes have been fulfilled, and
it has been infinuated to them that Mr.
Clarkfon had not authority for making
any, they therefore beg to be informed,
whether fuch is the cafe or not, and that
the Directors will point out on what footing they are confidered.

" That health and life is valuable and
uncertain ; that notwithftanding they labor
under the misfortune of wanting education, their feelings are equally *acute* with
thofe of *white men*, and they have as
great an anxiety to lay a foundation for
their children's freedom and happinefs, as
any human being can poffefs. That they
believe the Directors wifh to make them
happy

happy, and that they think their fufferings are principally due to the conduct of the Company's Agents here, which they fuppofe has been partially reprefented to the Directors.

" That Mr. Clarkfon had promifed in Nova Scotia, among other things, they fhould be fupplied with every neceffary of life from the Company's ftores, at a moderate advance. of ten per cent. on the prime coft and charges. That while Mr. Clarkfon remained in the Colony they paid no more ; but fince then they have been charged upwards of 100 per cent. That they would not grumble even at that, if the worft of goods were not fold, and paltry advantages taken of them, particularly in the article of rum. That they had known by Mr. Dawes's order feveral puncheons filled up with thirty gallons of water each, and even, though thus reduced, fold to them at a more extravagant price than they had ever paid before.* " That

* This is perfectly true, but upon inveftigation, it appeared to proceed from *religious* motives ; Mr. Dawes faid, he ordered a *little* water to be put into each puncheon, from a fear the confumers would neglect to dilute the fpirit fufficiently. Had fuch a trick been played at a *Slave Factory*, how would it be conftrued ?

" That the only means they have of acquiring thofe goods, is by labouring in the Company's fervice, and even this they are deprived of, at the whim of Mr. Dawes, or any other Gentleman in office, which they confider a prodigious hardfhip, as it is the only refource whereby they can provide bread for their families; that out of mere pique feveral have been difcharged from fervice, and not permitted, even with their little favings, to purchafe provifions from the Company's ftore-houfe, the only one here.

" That Mr. Clarkfon informed them before he failed for England, the Company had been miftaken in the quantity of land they fuppofed themfelves poffeffed of, and in confequence only one fifth part of what was originally promifed them (the petitioners) could be at prefent performed; which quantity the Surveyor would deliver them in a fortnight at furtheft, but they fhould have the remainder at a future time.

" That they fhould have been fatisfied had they got one fifth part of their proportion (*in good land*) time enough to have prepared a crop for the enfuing

fuing year, but the rains are now commenced, and the Surveyor has not finifhed laying out the finall allotments, which
he might have done, had he not re-
linquifhed the work as foon as Mr.
Clarkfon failed; and the greater part of
thofe he has furveyed, are fo mountainous, barren and rocky, that it will be
impoffible ever to obtain a living from
them."

After mentioning many more trifling
complaints, and dwelling greatly on
the happinefs and profperity of their children, they conclude with words to this
effect.

" We will wait patiently till we hear
from you, becaufe we are perfuaded you
will do us juftice; and if your Honors
will enquire into our fufferings, com-
paffionate us, and grant us the privileges
we feel entitled to from Mr. Clarkfon's
promifes, we will continually offer up
our prayers for you, and endeavour to
imprefs upon the minds of our children,
the moft lafting fenfe of gratitude, &c.
&c."

This petition is figned by thirty one
of the moft refpectable Settlers in behalf of the whole; and they have
raifed

raifed a fmall fubfcription for fup-
porting their reprefentatives while in
England: 'tis to be hoped the Directors will pay attention to them, and
not fuffer themfelves to be biaffed by
the mif-reprefentations of one or two
plaufible individuals, who muft of courfe
fay all they are able in vindication of
their conduct, and who, we have reafon
to believe, from their hipocritical pre-
tenfions to religion, have acquired a great
afcendency over a few of the leading
Directors ;—but furely they will not be
fo forgetful of their own characters and
interefts, as to allow that afcendency to
operate againft honefty, truth and juftice,
and ruin the quiet and happinefs of a
thoufand fouls :——no! they muft be
ftrangely altered indeed, laying afide
their partiality for Eiopians, if they
do not poffefs too much probity to
hefitate a moment when it comes before
them.

Befides difpleafing the blacks, and
rendering them uneafy, Mr. Dawes is
at conftant variance with fome one, or
other of the officers, and fince I wrote
you laft, few days have pafs'd over
without fome frefh feud; one in particular is of fo extraordinary a nature
I muft

I muſt relate it, that you may have a
peep into the diſpoſition of our Governor.

Mr. S——— a ſurgeon, who came
out in the Sierra Leone Packet, was
two months here without a room to
lodge in on ſhore, which was attended
with great inconvenience to him, and
interfered conſiderably with his duty;
he, after ſome time, interceded with Mr.
Dawes to let him have a ſmall room
fitted up in our houſe, which he ſoon
got finiſhed, and removed into; the apart-
ment being very comfortable and ſnug,
Mr. Dawes took a fancy to it, and the
day after Mr. S——— had taken poſſeſſion,
without any apology or preface, ſent his
ſervant to demand the key; Mr. S———
was ſurpriſed at ſo uncouth and arbitrary
a proceeding, and did not feel inclined
to treat it with paſſive obedience, but gave
a poſitive refuſal; as ſuch rudeneſs merited; in conſequence, he was immediately diſmiſſed from the ſervice, and
here follows an accurate copy of his diſmiſſion.

Council,

Council, Free Town, 26th *April*, 1793.

SIR,

   I am defired to tranfmit the en-clofed refolution of Council to you,

   and am, Sir,

  Your obedient humble Servant,

 (figned) J. Strand, Secretary.

Refolved, that Mr. S——, who came out to this Colony as Surgeon in the Hon. the Sierra Leone Company's fer-vice, has pointedly refufed obedience to the commands of the Superinten-dant, he be difmiffed from the fervice, and that from this day he is no longer confidered as a fervant of the faid Com-pany.

  entered
  (figned) James Strand, Secretary.

Did you ever hear of any thing more ridiculoufly defpotic?—but mark the fe-quel; the day following Mr. Dawes at-tended by the Secretary and his (Mr. Dawes's) fervant, came to the Hummums, for by this name I muft tell you our houfe is known, I was fitting in the piazza reading; they took no notice of
me,

me, but Mr. S——— being prefent, the Governor addreffed him, and demanded the key of his room, which of courfe was not complied with; he then defired his fervant to break open the door, who immediately got to work, and would have done it, but was flily checked by Mr. Dawes, who with as little ceremony or preface as he had offended, went up to Mr. S———, and faid, " I am much concerned, Sir, for what has paffed, if you feel offended, I beg your pardon, I have been unwell, or would not have acted fo rudely ; I wanted your room, becaufe it was retired, that I might be a little quiet; pray, Sir, return my papers, and forget what has paffed, you will greatly oblige and make me happy by doing fo."

Mr. S——— heard this penitential confeffion with amazement, and replied,— " Had you afked me in a gentlemanlike manner for my room at firft, it would have been much at your fervice as it is now, I bear no malice—here are your papers."

I could fill up twenty pages was I to acquaint you with all the private quarrels of this fort: but as they can neither afford amufement or inftruction, it is beft to pafs them over in filence.

On

On the 25th of April we heard of the French King being maffacred, and that England had declared war againft the blood thirfty banditti, who have ufurped the reins of government in France This account came by the Swift Privateer Cutter of Briftol, to the Ifles de Lofs, where fhe deftroyed a French Factory, and made fome valuable reprifals.

His Majefty's frigate Orpheus, Captain Newcomb, Sea flower Cutter, Lieutenant Webber, and the African Queen, a fhip chartered by the Company, arrived here the beginning of laft month. Captain Newcomb, in his way out, touched at Senegal and Goree, and captured fix French fhips, four of which arrived fafe at this port, and have fince been condemned and fold at Bance Ifland; the other two were loft on the fhoals of Grandee.

The Orpheus came out to protect the Britifh trade on this part of the coaft of Africa, as did the Sea-flower, in fome meafure ; but fhe is only to run down the Coaft, and proceed to the Weft Indies. After remaining here a few days, they both went to leeward, unfortunately three or four days too late, or they would have

have intercepted a French Corfair that has fcowered the coaft from Cape Mount (about fifty leagues from hence) downwards, confiderably annoyed our trade, and taken eight valuable fhips clear away, it is fuppofed to Cayenne; fhe had captured many more, which have been retaken by the Sea-flower and Robuft (a Privateer from Liverpool); thefe two veffels, we hear, have conforted and gone to Old Calabar, where they expect to fall in with and take a large French Guineaman, that has twelve hundred flaves on board, and is juft ready to fail. One of the fhips they re-captured was fent in here. I have feen the mafter of her, who fays he never faw fuch a favage looking fet in his life, as were on board the Frenchman. They all had on horfemen's caps (having a tin plate in front, with the emblem of *Death's head and marrow bones*, and underneath infcribed, " Liberty, or Death)," a leather belt round their waift, with a brace of piftols, and a fabre ; and they looked fo dreadfully ferocious, that one would fuppofe them capable of eating every Englifhman they met with, *without salt or gravy*. Unluckily the Orpheus fprung her foremaft, which obliged her to give up purfuing thofe Republican ragamuffins, and returned here.

During

During her abfence, one of the moſt atrocious infringements on the liberty of Britiſh ſubjeꞔts, and the moſt daring extenſion of arrogated power that has yet occurred among us, was praꞔtiſed, by our Colonial Tribunal, on the perſons of three ſailors belonging to the African Queen.

Theſe thoughtleſs ſons of Neptune came on ſhore to regale themſelves with a walk while their maſter was away (I believe at Bance Iſland) and as they ſtrolled through the town, wantonly killed a duck belonging to one of the Settlers; they were immediately apprehended, and taken before the Chief Magiſtrate, who committed them to priſon, and the ſubſequent day they were tried, not by their Peers, but by *Judge* Mc Auley, and a *Jury of twelve blacks*, who, without any evidence or defence from the priſoners, found them guilty of ſtealing and killing the *duck*. The *ſelf-created Judge* then ſentenced one of them to receive thirty-nine laſhes by the common whipper, fined the other two in a ſum of money each, and ordered them to be confined in irons, on board the York, till their fines were paid.

Theſe ſentences were accordingly put in execution; poor Jack was dreadfully mortified

mortified at being whipped by a black man; but his punishment being soon over, I considered it the lightest, for his fellow sufferers were kept ironed in the close hold of a ship, already infested with disease, upwards of three weeks, till the Orpheus returned; when the master of the African Queen presented a petition from them to Captain Newcomb, who did not hesitate to interpose his authority. He came on shore, waited on the Governors, and without waiting for compliments or paying any himself, he demanded of them, by what authority they tried White Men, the subjects of Great Britain, by a *Jury of Blacks;* it was so novel a circumstance, that it struck him with astonishment. " By act of Parliament," answered Mr. M'Auley. " Shew me that Act of Parliament," replied Captain Newcomb; the Act for incorporating the Company being produced, Captain. Newcomb read it over carefully, and finding there was no sanction given for holding any Courts of the kind, exclaimed, " Your Act of Parliament mentions nothing of the sort—your Court is a mere usurpation, and a mockery on all law and justice, I desire the prisoners may be released instantly." This, you imagine, was very unpalatable language to our *mighty men;* but they were forced to stomach it, and comply with the orders of their superior.

It

It is much to be wifhed; a fhip of war was always ftationed here; the very fight of her would reftrain the exercife of fimilar abufes, or any extravagant ftretches of undelegated power.

The firft Sunday in every month is the day appointed for holding this *sham* Court, which, withal, ferves very well for regulating any internal quarrels or mifunderftandings among the Settlers, by whom it is credited ; but extending its functions beyond them, is moft iniquitous prefumption.

Letters arrived by the African Queen from Mr. Clarkfon, faying he was coming out immediately. The joy this news produced was of fhort continuance, and fuddenly damped by difpatches from the Directors, mentioning Mr. Clarkfon being *dismissed*, and fucceeded by Mr. Dawes. This cannot in any way be rationally accounted for, but it is univerfally fuppofed the Directors have been betrayed into an act fo prejudicial to their interefts, and the welfare of their Colony, by liftening to fome malicious, and cowardly reprefentations, fent home by certain perfons here, who are fully capable of affaffinating the moft immaculate character, if thereby they can acquire latitude for their boundlefs ambition,

ambition, or, for a moment, quench their unconfcionable thirft for power.

No language can perfectly defcribe how much the generality of people are cha-grined on this occafion; they have added to their petition the moft earneft folici-tation for Mr. Clarkfon to be fent out again.

Numbers, hopelefs of fuch an event, are about to quit the Colony, and ever fince the news tranfpired, they have harraffed Mr Dawes with infults, in hopes he may take it in his head to be difgufted and march off. They even went fo far as to write a letter, reminding him of the recent melancholy fate of Louis XVI. and threatning fomething fimilar to him, if he did not inftantly acquiefce with fome de-mand they made relating to provifions, and which I learn he complied with, with-out hefitation. I fhould not be furprifed, after obtaining one demand fo eafily, if they repeated their threats, until all the promifes made them were fulfilled : but they fay it was the want of provifions, that incited them to *frighten* the Governor, and they will now wait peaceably till their Deputies return from England, or till they know what the Directors mean to do for them.

It

It will be a monftrous pity if this Colony does not fucceed after the immenfe fum of money expended on it: the original theory of its eftablifhment (fo generally known) was praife-worthy and magnanimous, nor do I fuppofe fuch a fcheme by any means impracticable; but injudicious management, want of emthod, anarchy, perpetual cabals, and cavils, will thwart the wifeft and noblelt intentions, which I predict will be the cafe here, unlefs fome fpeedy falutary alterations are adopted; if the prefent fyltem is continued, not only the Settlers, but the Natives will be provoked; all kinds of confidence will ceafe, the Companys funds will be fruitlefsly exhaufted, and more than probable, before ten years, we may hear that the Colony is dwindled into a *common* flave factory: fome fituations make it necelfary for fuperiors to be feared, and all fituations require they fhould be beloved; but if the prefent managers continued here, their lifetimes, they will never experience the pleafure of the latter, or the honor of the former; and retire when they like, I very much queftion whether they will leave one friendly thought towards them behind: — for this (though an

idea,

idea, well meaning men would blufh to
fofter) muft enfue, where the feeds of dif-
fention and rancorous jealoufy are fowed
and encouraged by thofe whofe province
fhould be to fupprefs their growth.

The Amy it is faid will fail in a week,
fhe carries a fmall cargo of about 1500l.
value, a laughable return for upwards of
100,000l. Being the firft remittance, I
dare fay it will be well puffed off in your
news-papers; to fee one of thofe puffs
would put me in mind of a perfons, face
diftorted with a forced laugh, when the
heart felt nought but emotions of agony:
for here is a capital ftock of more than
200,000l. half expended, and this firft
harveft I fuppofe, will barely defray the
difburfements of fhipping, and carrying
itfelf; what is more lamentable, fuch as
it is cannot be often repeated, for the
property is moftly funk in fuch a way,
that no probable or real advantages can
ever revert from it, without the aid of
an immenfe fum moft judicioufly applied.

The periodical rains are juft com-
mencing, and feem to fet in very fevere,
but I am in hopes of efcaping its inclemency,

mency, being about to turn my back on them, and bid adieu to this diftracted land, fo you may probably hear of our arrival in England very fhortly after the receipt of this letter, although we are to take a round about voyage by way of Jamaica. Mr — had taken our paffage in the Amy, but the Difcontents about to leave the Colony, are fo numerous, that fhe will be greatly crowded, and as the Naffau has excellent accommodations, fails well and immediately, he thinks we will be more comfortable in her, and lefs liable to fall in with French Pirates, than we fhould in the former, which is a dull fluggifh vef-fel, though it is a prevailing opinion here, fhould fhe (the Amy) meet with a French man of war, fhe will be in no danger, as the National Convention have offered protection to all the Company's fhips; how true this may be, I cannot fay; but it is probable enough, as two of the Directors were fome time fince nominated Members of the Convention.

We are to fail in a day or two, and I am very much hurried in packing up, and preparing for our voyage, therefore muft bid you farewell, &c. &c.

LETTER

LETTER XIII.

Swan with Two Necks, Lad-lane,
LONDON, 11th *October*, 1793.

My dear Madam,

I haften to acquaint you, that after a paffage of nine weeks and four days, in the Alexander (Shaw) from Jamaica, we landed fafe at Dover, the 9th inftant. My heart jumped with joy, when I found myfelf once more treading the fod of Old England, which at one time during our voyage, I did not expeft would ever be the cafe, for an ill-natured contagious fever, (when we had been but a few days at fea), difcovered itfelf in the fhip, and, before it could be checked, fcourged almoft every perfon on board; however, by the fkill and vigilance of the fhip's furgeon, only one death happened. We had been out about three weeks, when it attacked me, and was it not for the good nurfing and attention I had from every one, particularly the Captain, Surgeon, and my own good man, in all human like-

likelihood I fhould have fallen a victim
to its barbarity ; indeed, Captain Shaw's
impartial kindnefs to his fick, was beyond
every thing I ever witneffed before, and
in my opinion, ftamps him a man of
genuine humanity.

Our fhip was armed with two and twenty guns, and had between fifty and fixty
men on board. We failed from Kingfton
the 3d of Auguft, and the following day
fell in with thirteen fail of Spanifh fhips,
under convoy of a frigate, who was fo
very negligent of her charge, as to permit
us to intercept feven of them, which, had
they been French, we muft have taken in
fpite of all fhe could have done, being at
that time fo far to leeward, as to be fcarcely
difcernable. A Liverpool fhip, bound
home, had joined them the preceding
day, and now begged to be taken under
our protection ; this was granted, and
fhe kept company with us until we got into the chops of the Channel.

The fever that infefted us, broke out
among her crew, and hurried a fourth of
their number into the other world. Here
Captain Shaw difplayed his humanity
again, in a high degree, by waiting feveral hours every day, and thus prolonging
our

our voyage, to the prejudice of his own interelt, merely for the purpofe of rendering them what affiftance he could ; had he not, their fituation would certainly have been extremely comfortlefs, as the calamity I have juft mentioned was aggravated by the fhip being fo leaky, that the mafter and crew had it frequently in contemplation to abandon her.

We had little bad or boifterous weather during our voyage, and the time pleafantly vanifhed after health was reftored in the fhip ; fcarcely two days paffed away without meeting one or more veffels ; we always brought them too, and although none of them were of the fort wifhed for, they amufed and furnifhed us with news of fome kind. Clearing fhip, when a ftrange fail was feen, as if we really expected a rencounter, and exercifing our guns, once or twice a week, with all the manœuvres practifed in an engagement, were fouices of amufement altogether new to me. At firft, when a broad fide was fired it operated like an electrical fhock, but habit foon made it familiar, and at laft I was lefs fenfible of vibration from it, than the awful tremendous thunder we oftentimes had off the coaft of America, which was more fevere by far, than any I ever heard on the

coaft

coaft of Africa. This being the fubftance of every thing worth notice on our way home, I fhall therefore turn back to my quiting Sierra Leone, and fay fomething of what occurred from that time till my departure from Jamaica.

We embarked and failed on the ninth of June; nothing could have reconciled me to the idea of taking my paffage in a flave fhip, but Mr. ——— being with me, for I always entertained moft horrid notions of being expofed to indelicacies, too offenfive for the eye of an Englifh woman, on board thefe fhips; however, I never was more agreeably difappointed in my life. In the centre of the fhip a barricado was run acrofs, to prevent any communication between the men and women; the men and boys occupied the forward part, and the women and girls, the after, fo I was only liable to fee the latter, who were full as well habited as they would have been in Africa, and I had very comfortable apartments in the round houfe, where I could retire, when I chofe to be alone.

Having heard fuch a vaft deal cf the ill treatment to flaves during the middle paffage, I did not omit to make the niceft

obfer-

obfervations in my power, and was I to give upon oath what thofe obfervations were, I would declare I had not the flighteft reafon to fufpect any inhumanity or mal-practice was fhewn towards them, through the whole voyage; on the contrary, I believe they experienced the utmoft kindnefs and care, and after a few days, when they had recovered from fea ficknefs, I never faw more figns of content and fatisfaction, among any fet of people, in their or any other country. We had not our compliment of flaves by one-third, confequently there was an abundance of room for them. Regularly every day their rooms were wafhed out, fprinkled with vinegar, and well dried with chafing difhes of coal; during this operation the flaves were kept on deck, where they were allowed to flay the whole day (when the weather would permit) if they liked it; in the morning before they came up, and in the evening, after they retired to reft, our deck was always fcrubed and fcowered fo clean that you might eat off it.

Their provifions were excellent, confifting of boiled rice and Englifh beans, fometimes feparate, fometimes mixed, cleanly dreffed, and relifhed with a piece of beef, falt fifh, or palm oil, the latter feemed

feemed generally to have the preference;
a fuperabundance of this was their conftant
breakfaft and fupper; between the two
meals each flave had a large brown bifcuit,
and commonly a dram of rum. Great
attention was paid the fick of which, however, there were few, a mefs of mutton,
fowl, or fome frefh meat, was daily prepared for them, and we arrived in Jamaica on the 13th of July, with the lofs
only of one boy who was ill before we
left the coaft, and the remainder of the
cargo in much higher health than when
they had embarked.

Whether flaves are equally well treated
in common, I cannot pretend to fay, but
when one recollects how much the mafters
are interefted in their well doing, it is natural to fuppofe fuch is the cafe, for felf-
intereft fo unalterably governs the human
heart, that it alone muft temper the barbarity of any man, and prevent him from
committing violence on, or mifufing his
own property, and every cargo of flaves is
more or lefs that of the fhip's mafter's.

A few days before our arrival at Kingfton, Mr. W—-lb—ce and Tom Paine were
burnt in effigy. It would have hurt me
had I feen the former coupled with fuch
an

an incendiary, and thus expofed to public
ignominy; for, in my confcience I believe
he was impelled by too keen notions of
humanity, and too zealous a defire of doing
good, to take fo active a part as he has
done for the abolition.

For a length of time I viewed the Slave
Trade with abhorrence—confidering it a
blemifh on every civilized nation that
countenanced or fupported it, and that this,
our happy enlightened country was more
efpecially ftigmatized for carrying it on,
than any other; but I am not afhamed to
confefs, thofe fentiments were the effect of
ignorance, and the prejudice of opinion,
imbibed by affociating with a circle of acquaintances, *bigoted for the abolition,* before
I had acquired information enough to form
any independent thoughts upon the fubject, and fo widely oppofite are my ideas
of the trade from what they were, hat I
now think it in no fhape objectionable either to morality or religion, but on the
contrary confiftent with both, while neither
are to be found in unhappy Africa; and
while three fourths of that populous country come into the world, like hogs or
fheep, fubject, at any moment, to be rob'd
of their lives by the other fourth, I fay,
while

while this is the cafe, I cannot think the
Slave Trade inconfiftent with any moral,
or religious law,—in place of invading
the happinefs of Africa, tends to promote
it, by pacifying the murdering, defpotic
Chieftains of that country, who only fpare
the lives of their vaffals from a defire of
acquiring the manufactures of this and
other nations, and by faving millions from
perdition, whofe future exiftence is rendered comfortable, by the cherifhing hands
of Chriftian mafters, who are not only
reftrained from exercifing any improper
or unjuft cruelties over their flaves, by
the fear of reciprocal injury, but by
the laws of the land, and their religious
tenets.

All the flaves I had an opportunity of
feeing in Jamaica, feemed vaftly well fatif-
fied, their condiions appeared to be far
preferable to what I expected, and they
difcovered more cheerfulnefs than I ever
obferved the Blacks fhew in Africa, unlefs
roufed by liquor.

The Kingfton markets are as abundantly
fupplied with vegetables, both in variety,
and quantity, as any I ever faw ; and. I
was informed, wholly from the induftry
of flaves at their by-hours, for their

own

own emolument ; and I further heard, that notwithftanding many of them have in this way, amaffed money enough to purchafe feveral flaves, yet few inftances occur where they fhew even a defire of ranfoming themfelves. This is not a matter of much aftonifhment, when we reflect how little flaves in our Iflands are embarraffed with worldly cares : that they are fed when hungry, cloathed when naked, and kindly nurfed, with every medical care, when fick, folely at their mafter's expence, who only exact honefty, and a reafonable tafk of labour in return, after which, if attended to, they have nothing to fear, but, on the contrary, are certain of being rewarded and encouraged by extraordinary indulgencies ; and when the thread of life is fpun out, they leave this world with the pleafing thoughts that an interefted, if not naturally humane and indulgent mafter or miftrefs will fupply their place, and prevent their children from experiencing any want of a father or mother's foftering hand.

How very few of our labouring poor can boaft, when their mortal bodies become tenants of the grave, that their children have fuch certain provifion fecured them, and probably thoufands and thoufands

thousands of themselves may go supper-
less to bed this very night, and rise to-
morrow, not knowing where to get a
breakfast, or without the means of acquiring a morsel of bread to allay the
gnawings of hunger—whether then are
their situations, or those of slaves, having
Christian masters, most preferable ? The
question, in my opinion, requires but little
consideration.

Pray do not misinterpret my arguments,
and suppose me a friend to slavery, or
wholly an enemy to abolishing the Slave
Trade ; least you should, I must explain
myself,—by declaring from my heart I
wish freedom to every creature formed
by God, who knows its value,—which
cannot be the case with those who have
not tasted its sweets; therefore, most af-
suredly, I must think favourably of the
Slave Trade, while those innate prejudices,
ignorance, superstition, and savageness,
overspread Africa ; and while the Africans feel no conviction by continuing it,
but remove those errors of nature, teach
them the purposes for which they were
created, the ignominy of trafficing in
their own flesh, and learn them to hold
the lives of their fellow mortals in higher
estimation, or even let me see a foundation
laid

laid, whereupon hopes itfelf may be
built of their becoming profelytes to the
doctrine of Abolition ; then, no perfon
on earth will rejoice more earneftly to
fee that trade fuppreffed in every fhape ;
nor do I apprehend it would be impracticable, or even difficult to effect it, for
I ftill admit what I faid upwards of two
years ago, to be ftrictly juft.—" That
Nature has not endowed the Africans
with capacities lefs fufceptible of improvement and cultivation, than any other
part of the human race,"—and I am fure
they thirft for literature ; therefore, if
feminaries were eftablifhed on different
parts of the coaft, and due attention paid
to the morals and manners of the rifing
generation, I do not queftion but their
geniuffes would ripen into ideas con-
genial with our own ; and that pofterity
would behold them, emerged from that
vortex of difgrace, in which they have
been overwhelmed fince time immemorial,
eftablifhing focial, political, and commercial connections throughout the globe,
and even fee them *blazing* among the
literati of their age.

I am heartily glad to get rid of this
fubject, and am furprifed how I came
to entangle myfelf in it : but truft no
expref-

expreffions have flipped from me which will reproach my humanity or fenfibility, for the wrongs of mankind; if there have, impute them to miftaken notions of happinefs and mifery, for I am not confcious of meaning ill.

You will obferve, I was in Jamaica from the 13th of July to the 3d of Auguft, and perhaps may expect fome opinion of the country, people's manners, &c. from me, but any remarks of mine cannot be otherwife than trifling and confined, as my ftay was too fhort, and Kingfton, with a little of its environs, were the only parts I had a chance of feeing.

Kingfton ftands on the brink of a bay which forms the harbour; its fituation is varied, being partly low and partly high. I fuppofe it to be about a mile in length, and rather more than half in depth; a regular well built town, with ftreets intercepting each other at right angles; but I think many of them quite too narrow for that climate. I am told it is the largeft, beft built, moft opulent, and populous town we have in the Weft-Indies. The merchants moftly have fmall country villas, within a couple of miles round, which are called Pens, whither they retire, between three

and

and four o'clock in the afternoon, when all bufinefs for the day is compleated.

I found the heat much more oppreffive than I ever felt it in Africa, where I was, including both voyages, upwards of two years, without perceiving my fkin in any way difcoloured by the weather, but before I had been in Kingfton a week, I was tan'd almoft as brown as a mulatto. This I charge in a great meafure to living on the fea fide, open to the violent breeze, which fometimes blew a very ftorm, and which, I am perfuaded, is intenfely acid, for I never could leave a key, knife, or any piece of fteel expofed to it for half an hour, without getting rufted. The people drefs moftly after the cuftom of this country, and their manners are much the fame, except in hofpitality, which furpaffes all I ever met with.

I ufed commonly to ride out from five to feven o'clock in the morning, and then return to breakfaft; in thofe rides I often obferved the country tore up into deep furrows, which I conjectured were paffages of rivulets dried up, but was informed they were occafioned by heavy inundations, during the rains; notwithftanding this, I found the roads remarkably
good,

good, particularly the road to Spanish
Town, which is, without exception, the
beft I ever travelled upon; but underftand, it was made at a prodigious expence, being a great part of the way
through a morafs, which laying to wind-
ward of Spanish Town, muft contribute to
make that place very unwholefome; This
is the capital of Jamaica, about thirteen
miles from Kingfton, but in comparifon
with the latter, very infignificant; feveral
public offices, the affembly of the ifland,
and courts of juftice are held there; it
is alfo the refidence of the Governor,
whofe houfe is moft fpacious and elegant;* a marble ftatue of our late gallant Rodney is erected there, in memory of that ever famous action on the
12th of April, 1782; its ornamental effect is greatly loft by being placed in an
obfcure corner. I am much furprifed it
was not raifed at Kingfton, where certainly
it would have appeared to more advantage and notoriety; but the Houfe of Affembly determined that it fhould grace the
former, being the metropolis.

I have already told you what excellent
vegetable markets there are at Kingfton;
its flesh markets likewife are very good,
plenty of fat beef, but rather dark coloured

* It is faid to have coft 30,000l. Jamaica currency..21,428l. 11s. 6d. fterling.

ed and coarfe grained, excellent mutton, pork, and poultry of all kinds ; turtle in high perfection, and a variety of fine fiſh may be had every day.

Kingſton fwarmed with emigrants from St. Domingo, whofe miferies and misfortunes did not fail to draw compaffion and charity from its humane inhabitants, who fubfcribed moſt liberally to meliorate their fufferings, and I was credibly informed, that even the French prifoners have fo handfome an allowance as three and fixpence currency each per day, from the iſland of Jamaica, for their maintenance. Are not thefe proofs of generofity ? can a doubt exiſt that thofe people who not only affiſt the oppreffed and injured, but provide fo bountifully for their very enemies, are not alive to the niceſt definition of humanity ? only in minds warped by ignorance or prejudice, I prefume, and the opinions of fuch are very immaterial.

A very galling and extraordinary misfortune befel me while at Kingſton, which I cannot refrain mentioning to you. After we had been there about eight or ten days, a genteel dreffed man took lodgings in the fame houfe with us, and the following day we went to dine and ſtay the night

at

at a gentleman's in the country, when this
fellow availed himself of our abſence,
broke into my bed chamber, and rifled a
ſmall caſket, containing nearly all the
trinkets and valuables I had, to ſome conſiderable amount; be aſſured I felt prodi-
giouſly mortified at my loſs, which was not
a little aggravated by finding the knave had
eloped, leaving behind him, a trunk *half
full of stones*, in lieu of his ſpoils.

Tricks of this ſort occur ſo rarely there,
that it had made not a little noiſe, and the
Town Veſtry offering a handſome reward,
for apprehending the thief, I had the ſa-
tisfaƈtion of hearing, juſt before we failed,
that he was taken, but this was all, for he
had diſpoſed of what he ſtole from me, at
leaſt none of the articles were found in
his poſſeſſion ; however, it was ſuppoſed
he would be conviƈted of other burglaries
charged to him, and I cannot ſay, I ſhould
be hurt to hear, the world was rid of ſuch
a nuiſance.

I believe I have now noticed every circumſtance meriting attention, from the
time of leaving Sierra Leone, until our
arrival here, and having ſpun this letter
out to a greater length than was either ex-
peƈted or intended, I muſt therefore hurry

it

it to a conclufion, and fhall only obferve the Amy is arrived, with the two black Deputies from Sierra Leone, but I am not informed what kind of reception they have met with from the Directors, none of whom I have yet had the pleafure of feeing.

Mr.——— has fome bufinefs with them, which he is in hopes of accomplifhing fhortly, we then intend paying a vifit to you and the reft of my friends in Briftol.

Adieu,

Believe me always

Your's fincerely.

LETTER

LETTER XIV.

" Even the declarations made by themselves, eem wholly new and ſtrange to them; they forget not only what they have seen, but what they have said." **Wilberforce, on the Slave Trade.**
18th April, 1791.

LONDON, 23d *Dec.* 1793.

My dear Madam,

I Concluded my laſt by telling you Mr. —— had ſome buſineſs to ſettle with the Directors, part of which was on account of what they were, and yet are, indebted to me as the widow of Mr. Falconbridge, for money left in their hands, and for ſalary due to him when he died.

About a week after we came to town, I called at Mr. Henry Thornton's, but not finding him at home, left my addreſs, with a meſſage, that I wiſhed to ſee him on buſineſs. Several days elapſed without a ſyllable from Mr. Thornton, and conjecturing the ſervant might have omitted delivering either my card or meſſage, I called again, when his houſe-keeper
aſſured

affured me he had received both, but was then at his country feat at Clapham; I now left a note mentioning the circumftance of having waited on him twice, and beging to be acquainted when I could have the pleafure of feeing him; four or five days more paffed away without any anfwer, which puzzled me very much to account for. Unwilling, however, to nurfe any fufpicion that either infult or injury could poffibly be intended me, by a man who had fpontaneoufly made fuch declarations of friendfhip as Mr. Thornton did to me, before I went laft to Africa, and whofe charaƌer is currently reported, to poffefs as little alloy as frail man can be charged with, I therefore determined to venture another letter before I formed any opinion; the confequence of this was an anfwer that ftaggered me a vaft deal more than his filence; he informed me I would find him at his banking houfe, in Bartholomew lane, from ten to twelve the following day, if I *chofe to call there* I was vexed at receiving fo affronting a note from Mr. Thornton, becaufe it gave me room to queftion his veracity, and the Direƌors good intentions towards me; neverthelefs, a confciousnefs of having done nothing to merit fuch rudenefs, and my intereft requiring me to fee him, I curbed my

my nettled pride, collected as much compofure as it was poffible, and met the gentleman on his own ground. I believe he
neither expected or wifhed for this meeting; when I entered his counting room,
he blufhed confufion, and with fome difficulty he ftammered out, " pray madam,
what is your bufinefs with me ?" " I have
been induced to take much pains to fee
you Sir, to requeft you will get the Directors to fettle Mr. Falconbridge's accounts,
and pay what is owing me," anfwered I,
" why," faid he, " Mr. Falconbridge kept
no books, and he appears to be confiderably in debt to the Company." " Kept
no books, Sir, how can that be, when I
have a copy of them this moment in my
hands, a duplicate of which, I know your
Accountant at Sierra Leone (in whofe poffeffion the original books are) has fent the
Directors " " I have never feen them;
pray what is the amount of your demand ?"
replied Mr. Thornton. I then produced
an abftract account ftating the fum; " why"
fays he, its a large amount; I did know
Mr. Falconbridge left any money in ou.·
hands, I thought he had received it; and
his accounts for the Lapwing's firft voyage
were never fettled." This language ftart-
led me a good deal, but I refrefhed his
memory regarding the money left with the.
Direct-

Directors ; and told him he alſo laboured under a miſtake reſpecting the Lapwing's accounts, for he muſt recollect they were ſettled, and that he, fortunately, paid the ballance of 74l. 19s. 6d. to myſelf. Naked truths thus ſtaring him in the face, made him at a loſs what to ſay ; however after a little reflection, he told me, " whatever is due to you, madam, muſt be paid ; if you will walk into another room, and wait a few moments, I will ſend for Mr. Williams, the Secretary, who will ſee every thing ſet right."

I was then ſhewn into a large cold room, covered with painted floor cloth, where, after waiting ſome time half frozed, Mr. Williams came. His behaviour was gentlemanlike : when 1 had recapitulated nearly what I ſaid to Mr. Thornton, he enquired if Mr. Falconbridge left a will in my favour ? which having anſwered in the affirmative, he wiſhed me joy, as it would prevent others from ſharing of the little property he left—deſired me to get the will proved, and when that was done there would be no impediment whatever in my way, and I ſhould be paid immediately.

In a few days after, Mr. —— ſaw Mr. Williams, who told him, he had better
omit

omit proving the will till the Court exactly afcertained what amount I had to receive, as it would fave expence.

Perhaps Mr. Williams intended a kindnefs by this admonition, for he muft have known then, what I am now fure of, that the Directors mean, if they poffibly can, to withhold every fixpence from me; at leaft, there is great reafon to fuppofe fo from their quibbling conduct.

After detaining us here all this time, and fhuffling Mr. ——— off from one Court to another, without affigning any honeft, bufinefs like reafon, for doing fo; they now wind up their prevarications, by faying, they muft wait for further information from Sierra Leone, which I look upon tantamount to a pofitive refufal; indeed, it would have been much handfomer had they candidly declared at once, that it was not their intention to pay me—for their evafive anfwers have increafed the injury, by prolonging our ftay here to the overthrow of fome plans Mr. ——— had in contemplation.

What do you think of their charging me with the prefents they particularly directed, I fhould purchafe for, and make, Queen Naimbana; with the ftores granted
by

by the Court for me to take to Sierra
Leone, my journey to Briſtol and Falmouth, and every little donation they made,
either to Mr. Falconbridge, or myſelf.

But beſides theſe paltry, pitiful charges,
they bring forward three others of much
greater conſequence, though founded on
equally ſhameful and frivolous grounds,
viz. the Lapwing's cargo, with all the
expences of her firſt voyage, and for eight
months before ſhe left the river Thames ;
—the goods ſent in the Duke of Buccleugh, together with the freight and
paſſage money paid Meſſrs. Anderſon's,
and the Amy's cargo when we laſt went
to Africa.

They might, with as much propriety,
have included the whole of the Company's funds that have been thrown
away ;—yes, ſhamefully ſo,—no ſet of
raw boys juſt let looſe from ſchool,
could have diſpoſed of them more in-
judiciouſly.——What had Mr. Falconbridge to do with the diſburſement of
the Lapwing ? Her maſter was the of-
tenſible perſon. The trifling goods ſent
out in her and the Duke of Buccleugh,
were all appropriated conformable to the
inſtructions Mr. Falconbridge received ;
they

they were not intended for trading with, but merely as gifts of charity, and bribes, to pacify the covetous natives ; therefore, if Mr. Falconbridge had not accounted for them, it would be very eafy to find out whether they had been difpofed of that way : but I know every thing was fettled previous to our fecond voyage, and it is only a poor, mean fineffe in the Directors to fay otherwife.

As to the Amy's cargo, true—it was configned to Mr. Falconbridge; but that confignment was done away, when he received his frefh inftructions, after we arrived at Sierra Leone ; and before that veffel left Africa, the Mafter of her got a receipt for his whole cargo, from the Governor and Council, which receipt the Directors have at this moment.

I will not interrupt your time with this fubject longer than to give you the fentiments of the late Governor of Sierra Leone, who fays, in a letter of the 15th inftant, to Mr. ———, " I am forry the Directors fhould give you fo much trouble, and particularly about the cargo of the Lapwing for her firft voyage. They certainly are unacquainted with the circumftances, and the fituation of Falconbridge.

bridge on his firſt voyage, or they would never be ſo minute, particularly with his widow, who experienced ſuch unheard of hardſhips.

"I hope I ſpeak truth, when I pronounce their late Commercial Agent an honeſt man, but a very unfortunate one, not in the leaſt calculated for the ſtation he filled, which men of diſcernment might have diſcovered at firſt view. I aſſure you, had I been on board the Lapwing, on her firſt voyage, by myſelf, in Sierra Leone river, without a perſon in the neighbourhood likely to befriend me (which was the caſe with Falconbridge), knowing the country as I do, I ſhould have thought myſelf extremely happy to have returned ſafe to my native country, without any cargo at all."

I ſhall now leave you to make what comments you pleaſe on the vexatious treatment I have received from thoſe Gentlemen, and to turn in your mind what my proſpeéts would have been had I come home implicitly confiding in the profuſion of friendly promiſes they be- ſtowed on me (unſought for) when laſt in England.

I cer-

I certainly had a right to build some expectations from them ; but in place of any, you find those *paragons of virtue and human excellence,* unwilling to do me common justice, refusing to pay me what is religiously my right—a little pittance, which God knows, I gave the highest price for!

However, if there is any comfort in having company in one's misfortunes, or ill usage, I have that satisfaction. —Their treatment to Mr. Clarkson (the late Governor), and others, has been highly discreditable, but their behaviour to the two Deputies from Sierra Leone, and consequently to all their constituents, is the most inconsistent part of their conduct, because any injury done them must annoy and jar the Company's interest.

These unfortunate oppressed people (the Deputies) have related to me most minutely every circumstance that has befallen them since their arrival in this country ; and, as you seem interested in their behalf, and desire to know what success they have met with, I will repeat their narrative nearly in their own words.

" We

" We landed *pennyless* at Portſmouth,"
I think they ſaid " the 16th of Auguſt,
but we had a ſmall bill on the Directors
for the amount of what our fellow ſuf-
ferers ſubſcribed before we left Free Town.
The Company's Agent at Portſmouth gave
us two guineas to pay our way here, which
were deducted from our bill when it was
paid. As ſoon as we came to Town, we
went to Mr. Thornton's houſe, and delivered our Petition to him, he read it
over, and ſeemed at firſt to be very kind,
and to compaſſionate us very much, but,
in two or three days time, he told us the
Directors had received letters from Africa,
ſtating that our complaints were frivolous
and ill grounded. After this we ſaw ſeveral of the Directors, who told us the
ſame. We aſked who the letters came
from, but this they would not tell, however we are ſure Dawes and Mc Auley
are the authors, becauſe they muſt write
all the ———— they can think of to ex-
cuſe themſelves.

" When we had been here about three
weeks, finding our money almoſt ex-
hauſted, we applied to two of the Directors, namely, Mr. Thornton and Mr.
Parker, and requeſted them to ſupply us
with a little." The latter ſaid, " Yes,
I will

I will let you have money, if you will mortgage, or fell the lands due you by the Company," but the former had *more humanity*, he recommended us to go and labour for our fupport. To this we replied, we were willing to work, if we knew where to get employment.— Mr. Thornton then faid, ' You fhall be at no lofs for that, I will give you a line to a perfon who will employ you.'—" This we gladly accepted of, and accordingly got into fervice, where we wrought for near a month, without hearing the moft diftant hint of an anfwer to our Petition. We then began to grow very uneafy, and quite at a lofs what to do, having no friend to advife us.

" The Directors never would give us Mr. Clarkfon's addrefs, though we afked for it frequently; however, in the midft of our diftrefs, accidentally hearing he lived at Wifbeach, we wrote him without hefitation, enclofed a copy of our Petition, requefted he would interpofe his influence with the Directors, and in vindication of his character, endeavour to get juftice done us. We told him, all we required was the fulfilment of his promifes, which the Gentlemen at Sierra Leone had affured us he made without authority.

authority. When Mr. Clarkſon received this letter, he wrote to Mr. Thornton, beging the Directors would appoint ſome early day to meet him and us together, that he might explain his promiſes, and thereby acquit himſelf from having acted diſhonorable, in any ſhape, to the people he carried from America to Sierra Leone.

"We ſuppoſe the Directors did not like to ſee Mr. Clarkſon and us face to to face, for Mr. Thornton never anſwered that letter, which obliged Mr. Clarkſon to write another; this he ſent uſſealed, under cover to us, that we might be convinced of his good intentions and integrity towards us."

They ſhewed me a copy of the letter, which having read, I alſo tranſcribed, as I now do again word for word.

WISBEACH,

" *My dear Sir,*

"AS you have given me no anfwer to my letter, wherein I requefted a day to be appointed for the Directors, myfelf, with Meffrs. Anderfon and Perkins, the Deputies appointed by the inhabitants of Free Town to meet, to explain the promifes you authorifed me to make them, I am induced to take this method to convince the people at large of your Colony, that I have done all in my power, fince I have been in England, to forward the performance of the promifes I made them, with as much zeal as I ufed when I was on the fpot; and as I cannot bear to be fufpected by them, or the inhabitants of Nova Scotia, who were witneffes of my exertions in their behalf, I am induced to take this method of affuring them of the fincerity of my profeffions, as well that the promifes I made them were from the Directors of the Sierra Leone Company, and that they have as great a right to the performances of them as they have to difpofe of their own property.

" I fend

" I fend this letter to you (unfealed) under cover to Meffrs. Anderfon and Perkins, for their perufal, that they may affure thofe they reprefent, I have done all in my power to perform my engagements with them, confiftent with honour and honefty.

I am, Dear Sir,

Your's fincerely,

(figned)   JOHN CLARKSON.

To Henry Thornton, Efq.
Chairman of the Court
of Directors of the Sierra
Leone Company, London."

" We attended," continued the fpokef-man, " the firft Court after receiving this letter, and delivered it. The Directors did not feem well pleafed, but they made no obfervations on it to us. Before we left the Court, we were informed one of the Company's fhips was to fail for Sierra Leone immediately—that we were to return in her, and when *embarked,* we fhould have an anfwer to our peti-tion.

" We

" We thought it very ftrange, they
fhould put off giving us an anfwer till
we had embarked, and therefore objected, faying, we wifhed not only to
have, but to confider, the anfwer before
we left this country, and were proceeding to fay much more, when the Court
prevented us, by faying, " Whatever objections you have to make, or whatever
you wifh to tell us, you muft do it in
writing."—In confequence whereof, on
the next Court day, we prefented an Addrefs as follows :

" To the Honourable the Chairman and
Court of Directors of the Sierra Leone
Company.

" *Honourable Sirs,*

" YOU have defired us to com-
mit to writing what we wifh to tell you.

" We did not think, Gentlemen, any
thing more was neceffary than the petition
we brought, and delivered to you from
the people we reprefent ; but as you do
not feem to treat that petition with the
attention we expected, you oblige us to
fay fomething more on the fubject, for we
would be very remifs were we to leave
this

this country, without doing all in our power to get fome fatisfaction, not for the trouble we have been at, but fuch as will be pleafing and comfortable to our countrymen, and at the fame time ferviceable to your intereft.

" The Settlers at Free Town (thofe brought from America we mean), whofe thoughts we now fpeak, always believed the promifes made them by Mr. Clark-fon, in Nova Scotia, were your promifes. We are now convinced of the truth of this, by the letter from Mr. Clarkfon, which we delivered you on Friday laft.

" We certainly hope your Honors in-tend making good thofe promifes, and we beg to know whether you do or not?—We beg to have Grants for the land we at prefent occupy, and a promife in writing for the remainder, or the value, to be given at a future time named in that inftrument of writing.

" When we are able, we fhall confider ourfelves bound to contribute what we can, towards defraying the expences of the Co-lony; but this never can be the cafe until your promifes are fulfilled to us ; at pre-fent you are obliged to give us daily wages
to

to do work, from which no advantage can ever be derived, either to the Company or the Settlers; and we have no choice, but to do this work, or ſtarve; whereas if we had our lands, and that ſupport from the Company, which was promiſed, there would be no neceſſity for employing us except at ſuch work as was really wanting; and we might do as we pleaſe, either work on our own lands, or the Company's, whereby there would be a mutual advantage, and in a few years, with induſtry and good management on our parts, the produce of thoſe lands would yield a profitable trade to the Company, and we ſhould have the pleaſure of knowing we were providing comfort for our children after us.

" We always ſuppoſed we were ſent from Nova Scotia to Sierra Leone, by his Majeſty, (God bleſs him) the King of this Country; who, no doubt, expected our ſituation would be made better, from the aſſurances he had received of what your Honors were to do for us. We wiſh the Governor of our Colony ſhould be appointed by his Majeſty, whoſe ſubjects we conſider ourſelves, and to whom we ſhall be happy at all times of ſhewing our loyalty and attachment.

If

" If we are not of importance enough to this Country, to deferve a Governor authorifed by the King, we, with due refpect to your Honors, think we have a right to a voice, in naming the man who fhall govern us, but by this we do not mean to fay, that we have a right to interfere with the perfon whom you may chufe to direct or manage your property.

" We *will not* be governed by your prefent Agents in Africa, nor can we think of fubmitting our grievances to them, which we underftand is the intention of your Honors, for it is inconfiftent to fuppofe juftice will be fhewn us, by the men who have injured us, and we cannot help expreffing our furprife that you fhould even hint fuch a thing.

" Our Countrymen have told you, in the petition we delivered to his Honor the Chairman, — they will wait patiently till we returned, that their religion made them bear the impofitions of your Council, and prevented them from doing any thing that might be confidered improper, till they heard from your Honors, being convinced they would then have juftice fhewn them ; but we are forry to fay, we do not think you feem difpofed to

liften

to liften to our complaints, and if we are obliged to return to Sierra Leone, impreffed with thofe fentiments, and without obtaining any fatisfactory anfwer to the complaints and reprefentations we have made, it is impoffible for us to fay what the confequences may be, but we will make bold and tell your Honors, on the fwer we get, *depends the fuccefs of your Colony.*

" We wifh to return to our families by the Amy, and therefore beg to have your anfwer time enough for us to confider on it, before we leave this Country.

" We hope your Honors will not think we have faid any thing here but what is refpectful and proper; we thought it our duty to tell you the truth; we want nothing but juftice, which cannot furely be refufed us. We have been fo often deceived by white people, that we are jealous when they make any promifes, and uneafily wait till we fee what they will come to.

" We fhall conclude gentlemen, by obferving, fince we arrived here, we have avoided giving you trouble as much as poffible; we did not come upon a childifh errand, but to reprefent the grievances and fufferings of a thoufand fouls.

" We

" We expected to have had some more
attention paid to our complaints, but
the manner you have treated us, has been
just the same as if we were *Slaves*, come
to tell our masters, of the cruelties and se-
vere behaviour of an *Overseer*.

" You will pardon us gentlemen, for
speaking so plain; however, we do not
think your conduct has proceeded from
any inclination to wrong us, but from
the influence and misrepresentations of
evil minded men, whose baseness will
some day or other be discovered to you,
for the Great Disposer of events will not
suffer them to be hidden long.

We are Gentlemen,

With all possible respect,

Your faithful Servants,

(Signed) ISAAC ANDERSON. { Representa-
          CATO PERKINS.   tives for the
                             Inhabitants
                             of Free
                             Town.

" When they had read this over, they
" seemed very much out of humor, and
" we were desired to leave the Court
" room, but in a few minutes Mr. Thorn-
" ton sent us this letter."

" Messrs

" Meffrs. Anderfon and Perkins.

     " In confequence of an addrefs
" fent by you to the Court of Directors
" this day, I defire to be informed in writ-
" ing, what are thofe promifes of Mr.
" Clarkfon, which you fay, were made to
" you, in Nova Scotia, and are ftill un-
" filled.

I am,

Your obedient humble fervant,

(Signed)   H. THORNTON."

SIERRA LEONE HOUSE,
19*th Nov.* 1793.

" Here is our anfwer to Mr. Thornton."

To HENRY THORNTON, Esq. Chairman,
of the Court of Directors of the Sierra
Leone Company.

    "Sir,

     " AS you defire to be informed
in writing, what were the promifes made
by Mr. Clarkfon to us (the inhabitants of
Free Town) in Nova Scotia, we have to
acquaint you, they were to the following
purpofe :

     " That

" That his Majefty having heard of the abufes we met with in America, and having confidered our loyalty and fervices, in the late war, wifhed to make fome amends, and propofed, if we were inclined to go to Africa, we fhould be carried thither free of expence.

" That the part of Africa we were to be carried to, was called Sierra Leone, where a Company of the moft refpectable gentlemen, in England, intended to form a fettlement for the purpofe of abolifhing the Slave Trade.

" That he (Mr. Clarkfon) was authorifed by the Directors of that Company, to fay, each head of a family fhould have a grant of not lefs than twenty acres of land, for him or herfelf; ten acres for a wife, and five acres for each child.

" That thofe grants fhould be given directly on our arrival in Africa, free of any expence or charge whatever.

" That we fhould be provided with all tools wanted for cultivation, and likewife the comforts and neceffaries of life, from the Company's ftores, at a reafonable rate, fuch as about ten per cent. advance, upon
the

the prime coſt and charges, and ſhould not be diſtreſſed for the payment of ſuch goods, until enabled by the produce of our lands; but when we became comfortably ſettled, we ſhould be ſubject to ſuch charges and obligations as would tend to the general good of the Colony.

" That we ſhould be protected by the laws of Great Britain, and juſtice ſhould be indiſcriminately ſhewn Whites and Blacks.

" As far as we can recollect thoſe are the heads of Mr. Clarkſon's promiſes to us; almoſt the whole of which remain unfulfilled. There has been one fifth part of the lands diſtributed to moſt of the ſettlers, but they are in general, ſo mountainous, barren, and rocky, as to be of little or no uſe to them; nor was the ſurveying of that fifth part compleated when we left Sierra Leone, at which time the rains had ſet in, therefore it was impoſſible to clear or make much progreſs this year, and you muſt be ſenſible, Sir, of the injury we ſuſtain by looſing two years in the improvement of thoſe lands.

" We are charged extravagantly for all the goods we purchaſe from the ſtores, which

which we confider, not only a breach of promife, but an unjuft and cruel way of impofing a tax on us.

" We certainly are not protected by the laws of Great Britain, having neither Courts of Juftice, or officers appointed by authority of this government. But even the Police which we have formed among ourfelves, has not diftributed juftice impartially to Blacks and Whites, due, as we fuppofe, to the influence of your Agents; and we think it an unfufferable cruelty, that at the caprice or whim of any Gentlemen in office, at Free Town, we, or any of us, fhould be fubject, not only to be turned away from the fervice, but prevented from purchafing the common neceffaries from the Company's ftores, for the fupport of our families, while it is not in our power to procure them by any other mode.

We are Sir,

    Refpectfully,

       Your obedient, humble fervant,

(Signed) ISAAC ANDERSON, ⎱ Reprefenta-
         CATO PERKINS. ⎰ tives for the
LONDON, 20th Nov. 1793.   People of Free Town."

                      What

"What was the confequence of this letter? faid I—"Why the Directors were
no better pleafed with it than the firft, they
feemed quite in a quandary; were very
anxious to know whether any perfon had
affifted us in collecting and reducing our
thoughts to writing, interrogated us fepa-
rately on the fubject, and appeared greatly
difappointed with our anfwers."

"Have you had any anfwer from them?"
"No, Madam, and imagine they do not intend giving any; indeed we have heard
that they mean to keep us from going to
Sierra Leone again; if fo, it no doubt is
a ftratagem, to dupe and lull our Countrymen, who have faid they will wait peaceable, until we return; but fuch a poor little artifice is fo very unbecoming the characters of gentlemen, that we can hardly
believe it; however, if it is the cafe it
cannot avail much, and will in the end,
do them more injury than us; we have already wrote to our brethren, warning them
of our fufpicions, and guarding them againft
figning any paper or inftrument of writing,
as we have reafon to think fome thing of
the fort will be afked of them, to contradict what we have done; it will be a great
hardfhip on us to be kept here from our
families, yet, if it ultimately tends to obtain

tain juftice for our conftituents, or to fecure freedom and happinefs to them and
their children, we fhall think it no facrifice."

This is fully the fubftance of the informa
tion I have from time to time had, from the
two Deputies.*

Is it not almoft incomprehenfible that
Thirteen Men, whofe reputations in private
life (one or two excepted have hitherto
been efteemed fo fpotlefs, that the tarnifh-
ing blafts of fame, or the venom'd fhafts
of malevolence, have feldom ventured to
attack them, fhould, as a corporation, act
incompatible with common fenfe and common ———— ?

The Directors conduct muft really be a
fubject of confternation wherever it is
known

* Thofe two men returned to Sierra Leone, in
February or March laft, but two others have arrived
on the fame errand, and are juft now (Auguft, 1794)
in London : I am told they have many new complaints, among which is one of a ferious nature, viz.
That an enormous annual tax of two bufhels of neat
rice, equal to 130lb. has been demanded per acre
for their lands, notwithftanding thofe lands were
promifed them, *free of every expence, or charge
whatever.* Now, rice is fold from the Company's
ftore-houfe, at Sierra Leone, at the rate of fixteen
and eight-pence per hundred pounds, confequently
this tax would amount to 21s. 8d. per acre.

known; and fhould they not, of their own accord, fulfill Mr. Clarkfon's promifes to their fettlers, which they certainly feem inclinable to, I really think, in my humble opinion, this government ought to feel it a National concern, and enforce a performance.

His Majefty, no doubt, expe=ed he was doing thofe poor people an a=ual fervice, by removing them to a country, which gave birth, not only to their fore-fathers, but many of themfelves, and more efpecially fo as they were to be taken under the wing and prote=ion of fuch patrons of humanity, as the gentlemen condu=ing the affairs of the Sierra Leone Company *profeffed* themfelves to be, otherwife, he never would have hazarded their happinefs, by taking them from America, where they were moftly comfortably fettled;—where they might have been ufeful and valuable fubje=s, and where they had been, long before their removal, really an acquifition, befides fubje=ing this Country to the expence of upwards of 20,000l. for their tranfportation.*

Do you not think that immacculate Member of the Houfe of Commons, who is

* Thofe are a part of the very people, whom America (it is faid) is afking compenfation for.

is obftinately perfifting to abolifh the Slave Trade, would be better employed, and would difcover more real humanity, if he exerted himfelf in getting juftice done thefe poor blacks, whofe happinefs and comfort he has in fome meafure, though innocently, been the means of deftroying ?

Until all the promifes made them are performed, or, at leaft, a fincere inclination fhewn to perform them, no kind of confidence can exift between the Company and the Colonifts ; and, unlefs that is quickly fecured, the Colony muft fall to nought. It may not be amifs here to give you the fentiments of a Gentleman, zealous for its fuccefs, and intimately acquainted with the Directors, and with the progrefs of the Colony, from its birth.

He fays, in a letter to a friend of his at Sierra Leone, " I am fearful your prefent " Governors will forget the fituation the " Nova Scotians were in formerly ; the " number of times they have been de- " ceived, and will not make allowances " for the great change they have made ; " and I am more fearful of their not hav- " ing patience or moderation enough to " put up with their ignorance. It is an " eafy

(274)

" eafy thing for the Governor and Coun-
" cil to leave them to themfelves, if
" they are wickedly inclined ; but I
" I fhould confider fuch behaviour as
" the greateft fpecies of wickednefs on
" their parts, (the Governor and Council)
" and fhould think their education ill
" beftowed upon them, and their religion
" but fkin deep. What ! are they not
" fent out to inftruct them, and to fet a
" good example to the unenlightened
" Africans ? Ought they not to make the
" fame allowances for them as our fchool-
" mafters did for us in our infancy? and
" ought they not to know, that ignorant
" people, fituated as they are, with the
" bad example fet before their eyes by
" thofe who were fent out to inftruct
" them at the commencement of the
" Colony—are liable to be riotous and
" unruly—particularly when fo many
" have refided together, and but little em.
" ployment to keep their minds amufed ?
" with the promifes made them by the
" Company entirely neglected, and not
" the leaft appearance of a fpeedy com-
" pletion, or even a *defire* to perform
" them. I fay, had the Nova Scotians
" acted different from what they have
" done, under all thefe circumftances,
" it would have aftonifhed me, and I
" fhould have requefted thofe, who con-
                              " fider

" fider themfelves more enlightened, and
" ftood forward as their friends and pro-
" tectors, to have taken a leffon from fo
" fingular an example.

" Should you quarrel with the Nova
" Scotians, who do you think I fhall
" blame? Your Government and the
" Company ;—your *Government*, for want
" of patience, and for not fhewing an
" inclination to perform promifes, which
" will always fet ignorant people at va-
" riance with their leaders, and particu-
" larly thofe who have been fo often de-
" ceived before ; and the *Company*, for not
" enforcing their orders relative to pro-
" mifes, and for their dilatory manner of
" fending out the means to perform them
" with difpatch.

" If you fhould have a war with the
" Natives, it will certainly be the fault
" of your Government ; becaufe, you
" have it in your power, by a particular
" conduct, to make your Colony unani-
" mous,—and then you have nothing to
" fear.—You can always keep the natives
" quiet, if you have peace at home, which
" you may do, and at the fame time gain
" their efteem and confidence ; and if
" your Government fhould not, in every
" inftance,

"inſtance, do their utmoſt to preſerve
"peace and harmony, and make every
"degree of allowance for the ignorance
"and bad example hitherto ſet to the
"poor natives, and, I may add, the Nova
"Scotians, they will, in my opinion, have
"a greater crime to anſwer for, than they
"may be aware of—for ſhould your Co-
"lony, from bad management not ſuc-
"ceed, after *all the advantages it has had,*
"the friends to the civilization of Africa,
"will have reaſon to repent of their hav-
"ing made an attempt to inſtruct that
"unenlightened part of ſociety; it will
"depreſs the ſpirits of thoſe whoſe hearts
"were warmly engaged in the cauſe, and
"deter them from making future at-
"tempts.

"Theſe conſiderations have been ſo
"forcibly impreſſed on my mind, that I
"do not remember, ſince my arrival in
"England, of having ever written to, or
"converſed with the Directors, either as a
"body, or in private; but I have taken
"care to enforce, in as ſtrong language as
"I could, the neceſſity of performing, as
"ſoon as poſſible, their promiſes to the
"Nova Scotians.

⸎ ⸎ ⸎ ⸎ ⸎ ⸎ ⸎ ⸎ ⸎ ⸎ ⸎ ⸎

"I

" I have been almoft ready to expofe
" people who are deferving of blame, but
" the fituation of the Colony is fuch, that
" I am obliged to be filent, for it has many
" enemies in this Country, who would be
" rejoiced at having an opportunity to
" prejudice the minds of the Subfcribers,
" againft the meafures adopted by the Di-
" rectors."

I have given you thofe extracts, corro-
borant to many affertions I have made,
that you may not impute any of them to a
wrong caufe ; and I muft give you another
from the fame letter, very interefting to
the company's fervants and officers employed in the Colony.

" I find there is a religious influence in
" the Colony, that will carry every thing
" their own way with a majority of the
" prefent Directors, and whatever they
" fay, will be a law with them; and I
" really believe, that religion, which ought
" to have been the fupport and fheet an-
" chor of the Colony, will be its ruin,
" from its being practifed with too great
" enthufiafm and inconfiftency; and I am
" fearful, that thofe poffeffed of honeft
" hearts and independent fpirits, who will
" fpeak their fentiments as truth dictates,
" will

" will always be neglected by the Govern-
" ment there, and the Directors at home;
" and will never be done that juftice which
" their readinefs and exertions on every
" occafion to promote the profperity of
" the Colony, entitles them to."

Can the Company ever expect to profper,
or have officers of probity or worth, while
fuch is the cafe? No,—Sycophantic Hy-
pocrites are the only fervants who will continue in their fervice, and thofe will always
drain the purfes of their employers, by any
means, however fcandalous or difhonora-
ble, to fill their own.

ADIEU.

" To

To HENRY THORNTON, *Esq.* M. P.
*and Chairman of the Court of Directors of
the* Sierra Leone Company, *&c. &c.*

BRISTOL, *April* 4, 1794.

SIR,

BEING earneftly folicited, by feveral friends, to publifh the Hiftory of my *Two Voyages to Africa,* and having, with fome reluctance, confented, I feel it incumbent on me to addrefs this letter to you (which is hereafter intended for publication), by way of acquiting a tribute truth and candor demands, in fupport of what I have, neceffarily, mentioned regarding the Directors behaviour to me.

It is needlefs, Sir, to take a more diftant retrofpect of the fubject matter, than to the time of our arrival from Sierra Leone, in 1791.

If you will turn over to that period, and fearch into your perfonal behaviour, as well as the Court of Directors, to Mr. Falconbridge, I am perfuaded you will find it marked with repeated teftimonies

of

of approbation and applaufe, for the fervices you were pleafed to fay he had rendered the common intereft and original views of the Company.

For what purpofe did the Directors vote us a compenfation for our loffes? Or for what purpofe did they remove Mr. Falconbridge, out of his particular province as a medical man, and make him their Commercial Agent?

Were thefe not tokens of fatisfaction, and rewards for his extraordinary exertions to ferve the Company; or were they mere tricks of chichane and deception, to inveigle him to return to Africa, and anfwer the defirable end of fecuring a footing for the Emigrants, then expected from America? Let your own heart, Sir, decide upon thefe queftions.

I underftand the Directors perfift to fay, Mr. Falconbridge had not fettled the accounts of his firft voyage before he left England the fecond time; and that they impeach his memory, by faying he has not accounted for the cargo of the Amy, configned to him as Commercial Agent. Is it fo, Sir? Are thefe the paltry fubterfuges made ufe of for withholding

the

the poor pittance I am entitled to.—If they are? I fhall charitably fuppofe, for a moment, they proceed from error, and endeavour once more to fet you right,—though, believe me, not with the fmalleft expectation of profiting thereby.

To the firft I fhall obferve,—You muft labor under the misfortune of a very carelefs memory, if you cannot recollect that all Mr. Falconbridge's accounts, anteceding the 25th of December, 1791, were adjufted to that time, and that I received from *yourfelf* a balance of 74l. 19s. 6d. which appeared on the face of the account in his favor.

Can you deny the truth of this affertion, and fay there was no fuch fettlement? If you can, I will not attribute it to any harfher caufe than bad memory, for I yet think it is impoffible, Mr. Thornton would be fo pitiful, *willingly*, to utter an untruth.

But if this pointed circumftance had not happened, and I was wholly ignorant of the affair, I fhould fuppofe men of bufinefs (as fome of the Directors muft be) would never have fuffered him, or any perfon elfe, to commence the tranfac-

tions

tions of a new concern 'till thofe of the old were clearly concluded, but more efpecially fo in this inflance, as the charities Mr. Falconbridge had the diflribution of on his firlt voyage, were the property of the St. George's Bay Company, whofe original funds and effects were taken in account by the Sierra Leone Company, upon their incorporation, and therefore it was certainly neceffary that the Directors fhould be made acquainted with the true flate of their affairs.

To the fecond, I have to remind you, that Mr. Falconbridge never received the Cargo of the Amy, and confequently cannot account for what he was not in poffef-fion of; upon his arrival in Africa he got inftructions from the Directors, placing him entirely under the control of the Superintendant and Council, and the property of the Company folely under their direction, confequently the firft confignment and un-limited inflructions given him became nugatory; furthermore, the mafter of the Amy got a receipt for his whole Cargo from the Governor and Council, previous to his leaving Sierra Leone, which is juft now in poffeffion of the Directors.

Mr. Falconbridge had no independent authority or management over the com-

pany's

pany's goods after he received thofe inftructions, nor did he give any orders of
himfelf, as other hair-brained members of
council did, but got written inftructions
from the Superintendant and Council for
every fixpence worth he had. either from
fhip-board or elfe where, all of which is
accounted for in his books, delivered Mr.
Grey by the particular defire of Mr.
Dawes.

I am inclined to believe the Directors
are already acquainted with thefe circumftances, indeed it is almoft impoffible they
can be ignorant of them.

But admitting they are, what excufe
can they have for fwelling up an account
againft me with fictitious niggardly charges,
fuch as charging me with difburfements for
the Lapwing's firft voyage, not only during
her voyage, but for fix or feven months
before fhe left the river Thames. The
freight and paffage money of the Duke of
Buccleugh paid Meffrs. Anderfon. The
prefents I was defired to purchafe and make
Queen Naimbana, for which I have your
letter as authority. The ftores I was allowed to take with me for our ufe at Sierra
Leone. Our Journey to Briftol, Falmouth, &c. &c. ?

How

How can your *Honorable* Court, formed, as it is, of Members of Parliament, Bankers, and fome of the firft Merchants in the City of London, all profeffing the quinteffence of philanthropy, thus depreciate its worth by being guilty of fuch grofs meannefs? I verily believe it would be impoffible to cull from the Migratory Chapmen of *Rag Fair*, any number of men who would not blufh to be detected in a fimilar tranfaction.

That the Directors had caufe to be difpleafed with Mr. Falconbridge for not extending their commercial views, may be in fome meafure true; but tied up as he was, to obey the dictates of the Superintendant and Council, who would not liften to any arrangements of the kind, until comfort and regularity were eftablifhed in the Colony—What was he to do? however if he was altogether in fault, was he not punifhed by annulling his appointment as Commercial Agent? could the Directors do more? If they had blindly (as they certainly did in many inflances made improper appointments: What more could they do than annul them when they difcovered their miftake?

But I fhould fuppofe it did not require any great difcernment, to know
that

that a Surgeon, unacquainted with mercantile affairs, would make but as poor a figure in that line, as a Merchant, who had not ſtudied phyſic or anatomy, would make in the practice of ſurgery.

Mr. Falconbridge's diſmiſſion did not charge or accuſe him with any *crime*, but wanting knowledge cf his buſineſs; and what information the Directors could get on that ſcore muſt have been from a quarter as ignorant, if not more ſo than himſelf;—but ſurely, it was their province to have convinced themſelves, when they made the appointment, whether he was equal to it or not.

Did not Mr Falconbridge's diſiniſſion ſtipulate, that his ſalary was to continue till the Governor and Council procured him a paſſage to England? Could there have been the ſmalleſt idea, at that time, of detaining either the money left in the hands of the Directors, or his wages? Surely not.—Then why do the Directors now (he is no more) withhold payment from me ?

For ſhame, Mr. THORNTON, for ſhame ! ! !—How can you wink at my being ſo ſhabbily treated, after the un-
exampled

exampled fufferings I have undergone,
and after the prodigality of fair promifes
I had from you, to induce me to return a
fecond time to Africa Did you not tell
me, if any accident befell Falconbridge,
I fhould be handfomely provided for
by the Company? Surely, you cannot
forget making fuch a promife; — hich
you not only forego fulfilling, but fhame-
fully keep back (all I require of you)
the trifling fum fo juftly due to me.

If the Directors were not fearful of
fubjecting their conduct (towards me)
to the inveftigation of impartial men,
they never would have refufed fubmitting the affair to arbitration, as was offered; nor would they have threatened,
or boafted, that they would ruin me,
with an expenfive law-fuit, in Chancery,
when I fignified my intention of trying
the caufe at Common Law, if they meant
to do the fair thing.

I cannot help forming thofe conjectures, for how are we to calculate the
principles of men but by their actions?
Though, believe me, Mr. Thornton, notwithftanding all I have faid of the Court
of Directors, I yet firmly believe, if the
decifion was left wholly to yourfelf, I
fhould

fhould have ample juftice, and I cannot avoid thinking, from the opinion
I have heretofore formed of your benevo-
lence of heart, that you are fecretly
afhamed of the Directors nefarious treatment to me.

I will not trefpafs on your time any
longer, but fhall quit the fubject, with
refering my caufe to the loftieft of Tri-
bunals, where reigns a Judge of mercy,
vengeance, and juftice, who, I am perfuaded, will not let fuch turpitude go
unpunifhed, and who has, probably, already began to fhew his difpleafure.

Pray, Sir, receive this letter with
temper, and confider it comes from a
Woman, aggravated by infults and injury.

I am, &c. &c.

ANNA MARIA ———

Henry Thornton, Efq. M. P.
King's Arms Yard, Coleman-
ftreet, London.

F I N I S.